CREATIVITY BOOKS BY ED GLASSMAN

Creativity For College Students: A Frolicking Guide To Light Up Your Life" (2011).

"R&D Creativity & Innovation Handbook: A Practical Guide To Improve Creative Thinking and Innovation Success At Work" (2011).

"Team Creativity At Work-I. You Do Want To Be More Successful Than Your Competition, Don't You?" (2010).

"Team Creativity At Work-II. Brainstorming Isn't Creative Enough Anymore" (2010).

"Creativity Handbook: A Practical Guide To Shift Paradigms And Improve Creative Thinking At Work" (1996), a 250 page book written for his creativity workshops.

"The Creativity Factor: Unlocking the Potential of Your Team" (1991) San Diego, CA: Pfeiffer Books of University Associates.

"For Presidents Only: Unlocking the Creative Potential of Your Management Team" (1990) NYC: The Presidents Association of the American Management Association.

"CREATIVITY TRIGGERS FOR COLLEGE STUDENTS:
A Frolicking Guide To Light Up Your Life"

Ed Glassman, Ph.D.
Professor Emeritus
University of North Carolina
Chapel Hill

Former President, The Creativity College®,
A Division of Leadership Consulting Services, Inc.

Former Professor and Program Head
The Program For Team Effectiveness And Creativity
The University of North Carolina At Chapel Hill

Imagine YOU Shifting Paradigms in a Creative Climate using CREATIV-ITY TOOLS and TRIGGERS That Enhance CREATIVE THINKING and Solve Problems in an INNOVATIVE manner...
The Stuff That Dreams Are Made Of...

Brainstorming Isn't Creative Enough Anymore

-- CreateSpace --
https://www.createspace.com/3563703

SPECIAL THANKS

Joan Jolliffe earned my gratitude for editing my manuscript and civilizing it beyond my expectations. She did an excellent job and I appreciate it very much. Thank you, Joan.

However, all errors are still mine.

THIS BOOK IS DEDICATED TO:

- My friend, Vicki Bradley, who creates.
- My parents, who, in their own way, encouraged me to write this book when I was a child.
- My four daughters, Ellen, Marjorie, Lyn, and Susan, and their children, my grandchildren, Annie, Charlotte, Deborah, Dylan, Joshua, Julia, Nick, Rebekah, Sarah, and Trey.

ACKNOWLEDGEMENTS

My creative friend, Vicki Bradley, helped me in the presentation of numerous workshops. Much of the material in this book came from these workshops and the countless discussions she and I have had about creative thinking, especially hers.

In 1983, I was a Visiting Fellow at The Center For Creative Leadership in Greensboro, NC. Many professionals there helped to sow the seeds of this book. Some of these are: David Campbell, who inspired; Bob Dorn, who befriended; Bob Bailey, who clarified; Bill Drath, who helped me write better; and David DeVries, who advised with wisdom. I am grateful to all of them.

Many managers and professionals gave me feedback; to them I am very grateful. They are too numerous to mention but their input appears on many of these pages.

Finally, I want to thank the thousands of people who attended my workshops and kindly gave me feedback on what worked for them and what needed improvement. Without their input, I could not have continually improved and upgraded the workshop material that led to this book. I will always value and appreciate knowing them.

ABOUT THE AUTHOR

EDWARD GLASSMAN, Ph.D., former president of The Creativity College®, a division of Leadership Consulting Services, Inc. and Professor Emeritus of the University of North Carolina at Chapel Hill (retired), where he founded & headed The Program For Team Effectiveness And Creativity.

A Guggenheim Foundation Fellow and Visiting Professor at Stanford University (1968-69) and a Visiting Fellow at The Center For Creative Leadership in Greensboro, North Carolina (1986).

Professor Glassman's biography appeared in "Who's Who In America" and "Who's Who in the World."

He was an Educational Consultant for colleges and universities in North Carolina, California, Florida, Virginia, New York, and Canada.

Professor Glassman columns appeared in local newspapers on such topics as: "Business Creativity" and "Creativity at Work."

His articles on creative thinking and on team excellence appeared in Supervisory Management; R&D Management; Intrepreneurial Excellence; The Female Executive; Laboratory Management; Management Solutions; and The President.

His books on creativity and team excellence include:

• "R&D Creativity & Innovation Handbook: A Practical Guide To Improve Creative Thinking and Innovation At Work (2011).

• "Team Creativity At Work-I, You Do Want To Be More Successful Than Your Competition, Don't You?" (2010).

• "Team Creativity At Work-II. Brainstorming Isn't Creative Enough Anymore." (2010).

• "Creativity Handbook: A Practical Guide to Paradigm Shifts and Creative Thinking at Work," (1996) A 250 page manual used in his creativity workshops & meetings.

• "The Creativity Factor: Unlocking the Potential of Your Team," (1991) Pfeiffer & Company.

• "For Presidents Only: Unlocking The Creative Potential Of Your Management Team." (1990) The Presidents Association of The American Management Association, NY.

Born March 18, 1929, in NYC. He graduated from Stuyvesant High School in 1946, he received his Ph.D. in 1955 from the Biology Department, the Johns Hopkins University.

As a Professor in the University of North Carolina; Chapel Hill, NC, from 1960 to 1989, he published over 100 research articles on biochemistry, genetics, neuroscience, alcohol, teaching, and creativity.

He served on the Editorial Boards of 'Neurochemical Research' (1975-1978); 'Behavioral Biology' (1971-1976); 'Pharmacology, Biochemistry, and Behavior' (1973-1988); and 'Behavior Genetics' (1970-1971).

His experiences in colleges and universities as student, professor, educational & creativity consultant, his workshops, newspaper columns, and books provide the expertise to write this book.

PERTINENT ARTICLES AND BOOKS BY EDWARD GLASSMAN

(1982) A leadership skills program for scientist-supervisors. Laboratory Management (Sept), p. 46-49.

(1983) Your leadership style: How to capitalize on your subordinates' perceptions of you. Executive Female 6(5): 29-33 (Sept-October).

(1986) Creativity for greater productivity. Interview by Boardroom Reports (March 15), p. 3-4.

(1986) Leadership's styles effect on the creativity of employees. Management Solutions 31: 18-25.

(1986) Managing for creative thinking: Back to basics in R&D. R&D Management 16:175-183.

(1986) Habits that need changing. Intrapreneurial Excellence (June), p.4.

(1987) Your Leadership Style (in "Leadership," edited by A. D. Timpe. Volume 3 of 'The Arts and Science of Business Management'" published by Facts On File Publications, p 117-121.

(1988) Are your workers as creative as they could be? Management Solutions (Oct) p. 29-31.

(1989) Creative problem solving. Supervisory Management (Jan) p. 21-26.

(1989) Creative problem solving: Habits that need changing. Supervisory Management (Feb) p. 8-12.

(1989) Some triggers for problem solving. Supervisory Management (March) p.14-18.

(1989) Creative problem solving: Your role as leader. Supervisory Management,(April) p. 37-42.

(1989) Creative team building without a consultant. The President (published by the American Management Assoc.) 25 (No 8): Sept, p. 4.

(1990) "For Presidents Only: Unlocking the Creative Potential of Your Management Team." New York: Presidents Association, American Management Association.

(1990) Understanding and supervising low conformers. Supervisory Management 35 (November), p 10.

(1990) Leadership's styles effect on the creative thinking of employees. Pins and Needles National Productivity Board of Singapore. Issue 5:34-38.

(1991) "The Creativity Factor: Unlocking the Potential of Your Team." San Diego, CA: Pfeiffer Books of University Associates.

(1991) Selling your ideas to management. Supervisory Management 39: (Oct) p 9.

(1991) Self-directed team building without a consultant. Supervisory Management. (March) p. 6.

(1996) Creativity Handbook: A Practical Guide To Shift Paradigms And Improve Creative Thinking At Work, a 250- page book written for his creativity & innovation meetings & workshops.

(2010) Team Creativity At Work I. You Do Want To Be More Successful Than Your Competition, Don't You?

(2010) Team Creativity At Work II. Brainstorming Isn't Creative Enough Anymore.

(2010)   Two Interviews by Vern Burkhardt for IdeaConnection.com

http://www.ideaconnection.com/open-innovation-articles/002

20-Overcome-Mind-Funnels.html

http://www.ideaconnection.com/open-innovation-articles/00222-Trigge
r-Ideas-and-Metaphors.html?ref=nl110210

(2011) R&D Creativity & Innovation Handbook: A Practical Guide To Improve Creative Thinking and Innovation At Work.

TABLE OF CONTENTS

PART 3
SOLVE PROBLEMS CREATIVELY _ALONE_

Creativity produces golden thoughts, new & useful ideas.

Whether you are an undergraduate, a graduate student, or a student in a professional school, this book will help you change from a person that has to be reminded to 'think outside the box,' to a person who eliminates the box from your thinking, a person that spouts unexpected ideas generously, and solves problems creatively.

SAVOR YOUR CREATIVITY

I enjoy my creativity. Ideas pop into my head in an erratic stream. It adds spice to my life. And it enabled me to write this book and contribute to the quality and excitement of my life.

Savor your creativity. It will help you enjoy your life. To reveal some dimensions of your own creativity, finish these statements:

"When I am creating, I feel ..."

The biggest help to my creativity is ..."

The biggest obstacle to my creativity is ..."

I need the following to be more creative ..."

IF YOU ALWAYS DO WHAT YOU HAVE ALWAYS DONE,
YOU WILL ALWAYS GET WHAT YOU HAVE ALWAYS GOTTEN,
Maybe less...

Creative thinking fuels your ability to generate an unexpected "new and useful" idea. The more unexpected the idea, the more creative we perceive it.

Today the process works even better. No longer do we have to wait for someone's brain to slowly churn out a new and useful idea. Now we have hundreds of **creativity triggers** to help spark ideas to achieve high-quality solutions to problems.

"Hold on," you say. "Didn't the old methods work for thousands of years to produce ideas? Didn't we construct our entire civilization using those old ways? Why a new way? If it ain't broke, why fix it?"

Of course, the old ways still work. And we did construct our civilization slowly waiting for ideas to slowly appear.

Nonetheless, the new **creativity triggers** heat up the process, so we generate more new and useful ideas in a shorter time. And because we have more ideas to choose from, we turn out higher quality solutions, avoiding the quick fix.

Groups using brainstorming to generate ideas complain that they have trouble sorting and selecting so many ideas. How sweet to move beyond the old bottleneck of not having enough ideas to the problem of evaluating the myriad of ideas a simple brainstorming session produces.

And Alex Osborn invented brainstorming over 80 years ago, the era of the Model-A Ford and the DC-3 airplane. Not a modern procedure at all. Indeed, using only brainstorming today mimics driving around in a Model-A Ford or a DC-3 airplane, ignoring computers, antibiotics, TV, the Internet, the i-pad, mobile phones, and the thousands of modern inventions from which we benefit. You need to use modern creativity triggers.

This book focuses on what works, not theory. I presented workshops for over 15 years, and I learned that while theory helps us understand, creativity triggers that succeed help us even more.

I emphasize the following ways to use creativity triggers to solve problems creatively:

- to shift paradigms and produce unexpected, fresh ideas and solutions.

- to change the climate so new ideas flourish.

- to stop pigeonholing people and stifling their creative thinking.

I describe all three types of creativity triggers in this book. You will also find the following:

• Creativity triggers on an 8-rung problem solving ladder that carry out the three key creative rungs, shift paradigms, and achieve creative solutions.

• Creativity triggers to form permanent creativity groups from students in your college.

• Creativity triggers to motivate students to create creative outcomes that succeed.

• Creativity triggers to avoid habits that suppress creative thinking.

This book can work for you. The results ultimately depend on your commitment to alter habits and apply new creativity triggers to solving problems.

REDUCE YOUR RESISTANCE TO USING CREATIVITY TRIGGERS

Today, many people find that creative thinking contributes to a winning competitive edge. Students who work alone, or in groups, use creativity triggers to solve problems more creatively. Turn your complacency into dynamic creative outcomes.

Most students drop their resistance to creativity triggers once they accept some new ideas:

First, creative thinking involves an ordinary, daily activity. **S e c-ond**, students can learn creativity triggers. Using these triggers does not turn anyone into an Einstein, but they do help students find better solutions to problems.

Third, students can change the habits that spoil creative thinking and doom the creative climate.

Finally, students using creativity triggers can achieve quality solutions which lead to success.

Skeptical students need to discover that many ways exist to perceive a problem, that diverse solutions exist, and that using creativity triggers works, a key change in attitude.

This book will show you how to do it effectively.

CREATIVITY TRIGGERS DO HELP

Many students underestimate the power that creativity triggers provide, because they believe creative thinking comes from an exceptional, inherited gift. You either have it or you don't.

Not so. Most of us have creative ability and use it everyday. We don't recognize it as creativity or even see it as special. We call it tinkering, ingenuity, intuition, trial-and-error, imagination, making suggestions, inventing --- anything but creative thinking. We think creative thinking an exceptional gift inherited by other students.

Not true. Most students think creatively most of the time; it depends on what you spend your time creating that makes the difference. Best of all, creativity triggers helps solve problems more effectively in your life and your career.

We could not have survived as a species had we not been creative and adjusted to changing conditions.

Many levels of creative thinking exist, from low daily levels to hot, unexpected levels. To increase the probability you operate at a higher level use creativity triggers to analyze your problem, generate ideas, select solutions, and create a creative atmosphere in your mind without pigeonholing yourself or others.

• PART 1 •
CREATIVITY TRIGGERS

CHAPTER 1.
WHAT IS CREATIVITY?

The Mysterious Connectivity Of Creativity

According to the experts, creativity is the production of new and useful ideas. You accomplish this by *combining* old bits & pieces in your mind (and in your surroundings) into one thought to produce unexpected outcomes.

This process provokes the conversion of old ideas into new ideas. You do NOT create new ideas out of nothing. That doesn't happen.

For example: To invent a clock radio, you must know something about clocks and radios, and think about them in an environment that acts as a catalyst to combine the information into one thought.

Thus, to be creative, you need to have bits & pieces in your mind, and you have to establish an environment containing creativity triggers so a combination takes place. **Creativity triggers** are what most of this book is about. Use this approach to enhance your creativity.

What Are Creativity Triggers?

Casual creativity triggers vary widely. A chance remark. Deep focus on a problem. Deliberate thought and incubation. Meditation. Serious discussion with other people. Another person's idea. Dreaming. A shower. A walk in Nature. Riding quietly in a vehicle. Resting. Laughing. Having fun. A relaxed and quiet state. Excited.

These casual triggers succeed now and then to spark new ideas.

In addition, many **dozens** of not-so-casual advanced creativity triggers exist, like brainstorming and brainwriting, described in this book. These advanced creativity triggers target, focus, and speed up the creative process, so you do not have to wait around and hope for new ideas to appear.

How Do Creativity Triggers Work?

We do not know the neurological and physiological basis of creativity triggers. Their mode of operation is unknown. Each trigger has a sudden effect to spark and produce a new & useful idea.

Creativity triggers provoke new ideas that succeed or, failing that, add to the bits and pieces in your mind. This property makes them very useful.

SOME BASIC ELEMENTS IMBEDDED IN ADVANCED CREATIVITY TRIGGERS

Advanced creativity triggers contain **basic elements** and underlying principles. Once you appreciate their fine points, you can use them more effectively. You can even design your own creativity triggers by creatively combining elements from different triggers to fit special needs.

Seek Many Alternatives

During the creative process, whether you seek to analyze a problem, create an idea, find a blockbuster solution, you can avoid the 'quick fix' by generating many alternatives

Consider this situation. You perceive a problem you want to solve. An idea flashes through your mind. You like it. It appears to work. You shout eureka, and the creative process ends. Actually, it hardly started, because this is the quick fix.

The quick fix only scratches the surface of the alternative solutions available had you continued the creative process. The quick fix keeps you from a better alternative.

To avoid the quick fix, generate at least five new alternatives. One hundred is better, but who's counting.

Ignore Premature Criteria

Knowing the criteria for a quality solution too soon suppresses creative thinking. Criteria box you in, and you waste time worrying whether each idea and new perspective meets the criteria.

Instead, dump criteria. Distort, ignore, and forget stated and un-stated phantom criteria. Phantom criteria include those you made up or carry unawarely in your mind. You think they apply, but they don't. No one told you to use them. Reverse and twist the criteria in your mind to make them ineffectual.

Avoid Instant Evaluation

Evaluation depends on old ideas and old information. Creativity seeks new ideas and new information. Old and new conflict with each other. Evaluation versus the new idea.

So, to escape old thinking patterns, do NOT evaluate new ideas too soon. New ideas are often fragile petals that cannot survive the gaunt-let, the barrage of critical thinking. So please stop instant evaluation, the basis of your internal gauntlet.

Listen To Other People's Ideas

Other people's ideas will often trigger new ideas in you.

Forced-Withdrawal

Change the setting of your perspective. Create and combine alternatives within a different context than the real problem you want to solve.

For example, pretend that you attend a different school in a different country, or that you are a different person. Or solve a similar or related problem. In this way, you avoid getting bogged down in stifling old thoughts and habits.

Forced-withdrawal helps you escape some of the constraints of your problem and provides you a clearing within which to stay creative.

Trigger-Statements

Trigger-statements include problem-analyzing statements that will not work. However, when properly used as creativity triggers they will spark other problem-analyzing statements that shift paradigms and change perspectives. They help you avoid timeworn paradigms and lead you down new mental paths.

Trigger-Ideas

Ideas that do not contribute to a quality solution, when properly used, can trigger other ideas that do work. Trigger-ideas can play a key role in creative thinking.

Stay open to this possibility when pursuing a quality solution. Indeed, even indifferent, exotic words can spark new ideas.

Forced Combinations

You may create unexpected and useful ideas by combining ideas, objects, thoughts, and impressions with your problem statement. You may connect your problem with thoughts related or unrelated to the problem.

Combinations with **related** items yield less novel outcomes which are often easier to apply to the problem. Combinations with **unrelated**, distant items produce very creative results, though hard to apply to the problem. Take your choice, but why use advanced creativity triggers to produce prosaic results.

Idea Improvement

Improve your idea relentlessly. This process itself will spark many more new ideas.

1. List what you **like** about the idea so you won't change that.
2. List what needs **improvement**.

This process will give you a sense of the usefulness of your idea. To improve an idea in depth, list the following:

1. The characteristics and properties of the idea.
2. What's useful and what you like about the idea?
3. Deficiencies and what you do not like in the idea that need improving.
4. Ways to overcome deficiencies and improve your idea.

Recycle these four steps until the idea shines. This process acts like a creativity trigger, and will spark additional new alternatives throughout.

Personalize Your Creativity Triggers

Some people prefer to work in groups. Some people like to work alone. Some don't have a preference. Some people combine bits and basic elements from many creativity triggers into a trigger that works well for them. Mix & match.

Remember: what works counts, not what an expert prescribes.

Use Bizarre Ideas To Startle &
Upset Your Viewpoint

Generate a bizarre idea often to shake things up. See Chapter 5 for a full description of this element.

ADAPT CREATIVITY TRIGGERS TO YOUR
OWN NEEDS

Adapt the creativity triggers in this book to your use.
Stay creative when switching basic elements.
What works counts most. Avoid philosophical distractions.
Allow no boundary to limit how much you change a creativity trigger to fit what you want.
Avoid the internal gauntlet and other habits that distort the creative atmosphere in your mind.
Use forced-withdrawal with metaphors and analogies to let your subconscious mind creep in.
Stay patient and relentless.
Turn the creative process into an on-going habit.

INCUBATION AND OTHER STAGES
IN THE CREATIVE PROCESS

Some stages of the creative process include the following:

Preparation Stage: Fact finding; laying the groundwork and learning the background; learning the creative process.

Concentration Stage: Total absorption in the problem; trancing out.

Incubation Stage: Taking time out; resting; seeking distractions; working on other things; vacationing; jogging; taking walks; having fun.

Illumination Stage: The 'Ah-Ha' moment when the insight forms and ideas pop out.

Implementation Stage: Solving practical problems of implementation; getting other students involved. In other words, the hard work.

The **preparation** stage, is the time during which you fill your mind with new bits and pieces to make remote connections later. It can last many years; for example, the time spent in school, on-the-job training, reading, taking courses and workshops, using clever phones, traveling, life experiences, the internet, etc.

After all, you cannot be a creative chemist, engineer, or computer whiz unless you know chemistry, engineering, or computers. You learn your craft and profession first.

During the **concentration** stage, you focus on a particular problem or task, and absorb yourself in it, making a place in your mind for a new idea to enter.

Frustration at not finding a solution leads to the **incubation** stage, during which you concentrate on other things while your mind takes a break and quietly makes remote connections.

Then, if you are fortunate, the **illumination** stage occurs. The paradigm shifts, the 'Ah-Ha' insight forms, and a new idea emerges.

Then the **implementation** stage occurs, a stage that can last a short time or a lifetime, as the entire process cycles repeatedly to modify, implement, and develop the idea.

Thus, new ideas do not appear spontaneously out of the blue. They require preparation, concentration, incubation, and the appropriate creativity triggers to spark remote connections. This book will show you some powerful triggers.

When new ideas appear, they need special and deliberate nurturing, or they disappear.

These notions trigger a number of issues:
- How much incubation time do you build into your schedule? While working on a problem, would you spend a day or two walking in the woods or sitting on a beach?

- If someone sits with his or her feet on the desk looking out the window for several hours, or even days, would you find this behavior acceptable?

A HABIT THAT SPOILS CREATIVE THINKING: You do not allot enough time to the incubation stage of the creative process.

- Do you value "doing things" more highly than "thinking"? Is it okay for you to spend time thinking, or, seeming to do nothing?
- How much time do you allot to the preparation stage to get diverse bits & pieces into your mind?
- How do you obtain diverse bits and pieces for your mind? By taking classes, traveling, attending meetings or conventions, reading, using the computer? By talking to peers and faculty, to students in other schools, in foreign lands, in other majors? Does your college encourage this? Does your lifestyle allow this?

A HABIT THAT SPOILS CREATIVE THINKING: You do not increase the diverse pieces and bits in your mind.

PERSONAL ENVIRONMENTAL CREATIVITY TRIGGERS

Another way to help creative effort involves recognizing and deliberately using your personal creative environmental triggers that helps stimulate your creative juices. For example, some students respond to music, while others need absolute quiet when thinking creatively.

These conditions range from mild to seemingly outrageous behaviors. When these conditions exceed the level of tolerable low-conformity, other people exert pressure. Often, the person stops the behavior. In any case, creative thinking slows.

A TRUE STORY: In one of my creative thinking workshops, a participant told of going to his office on a Sunday morning, a rare event for him, and finding the person who shared his office working intensely with obvious relish at his desk in his underwear.

The coworker explained that he had discovered earlier in life that he worked best and stayed most creative while working in his underwear. So, he came to work on Sunday when he could work unbothered by others.

When I tell this true story, people report this type of behavior too bizarre and unacceptable (see 'leapers' in Appendix III). So, I offer other personal environments to ponder. Most come from "Stimulating Creative Thinking" by M. Stein (1975).

• Emile Zola worked at midday in artificial light.
• Lommenais worked in a room of shadowy darkness.
• Kipling wrote only with the blackest ink he could find.
• Ben Johnson performed best drinking tea while stimulated by the purring of a cat and the strong odor of orange peel.
• Schiller kept rotten apples in his desk and his feet in cold water.
• Shelley and Rousseau worked bareheaded in the sun.
• Boussuet worked in a cold room with his head wrapped in furs.
• Milton, Descartes, Leibnitz and Rossini lay stretched out.
• Tycho-Brache and Leibnitz worked secluded.
• Proust worked in a cork-lined room, Carlyle in a noise-proof room.
• Balzac wore monkish working garb and worked at night with strong, black coffee.
• Churchill, Frost, D'Annunzio, and Farnol worked best at night.
• Picasso painted best when someone else was in the studio.
• Guido Reni painted and de Musset wrote poetry best when   dressed in magnificent style.
• Mozart worked best following exercise.
• Wagner composed music best while stroking velvet.
• A writer of Jackie Gleason's TV show had his most creative moments in the bathroom.

Some students prefer sharpened pencils, a cleared desk, a disorderly room, quiet, music, or noise. Although personal creativity environments provide needed security, you may not carry out borderline behaviors fearing what others think.

A TRUE STORY: I get at least one good, unexpected idea while taking a shower, and I stay much more creative and productive if I read and write in bed as soon as I wake up without interacting with other people. In fact, I wrote this book while I stayed in bed every morning and started writing when I woke up, often without stopping through mid-afternoon. I listened to Puccini's operas and stayed most creative.

Have you discovered your own personal creativity environments? If you arrange these conditions, you might be able to make small changes that lead to great increases in your creative output.

A TRUE STORY: One person told me that he gets his best ideas in the middle of the night. To make sure he captures these ideas, he has a small light, pen and paper next to his bed so he can write them down. Many people tell me similar stories. Some tell me they get their best ideas when driving a car, some while taking a shower or a bath, some shortly after waking in the morning, and some when walking to work. Do you know when you get your best ideas? Do you arrange for these occasions to occur more frequently to help your creative outcomes?

Turn the creative process into an ongoing habit.

• CHAPTER 2 •
REASONS TO THINK CREATIVELY...NURTURE THE CREATIVE FLAME WITHIN

"The enjoyment of creative effort provides its own reward."

If you have drifted into routine ways, you might change your habits and use creativity triggers to help you improve your creative thinking and get you out of your ruts. The following may also indicate a need to boost the way you think:

• You always think the same way...or think very little.
• You keep doing the same things in the same ways.
• You lack interest in what you do.
• You don't take risks in your work.
• Your life does not challenge you enough.
• You ask few challenging questions.
• You have resistance to trying out something new.

This constitutes one reason to think creatively: to get out of ruts.

"When I Am Creative, I Feel..."

Let us return to how you feel when you engage in creative effort. If you haven't already done so, please finish this statement: "When I am creative. I feel..."

You probably wrote good feelings, such as: fulfilled, joyful, good, enthusiastic, insightful, stimulated, enjoyable, intense, fun, happy, delighted, good, satisfied, useful, energetic, alert, challenged, worthwhile, energized.

These word describe the feelings of enjoyment that most people describe when they are creative. This is an important reward of being creative.

Thus, one important reason to indulge in creative thinking is to enhance your enjoyment of life. So, go ahead, indulge yourself, and spend time frolicking with your creativity.

SUCCESS & CREATIVITY

Another reason to be creative is to help with success in your college career, your activities, your work, your relationships, and throughout your life. The creativity triggers described in this book will help you glide to your success, especially in view of the strains of the global economy.

By success I mean knowing and getting what you want. It's not simple or easy, but this book can help.

"The Biggest Help To My Creativity Is..."

If you haven't already done so, please finish this sentence: "The biggest help to my creativity is..."

You have a 50% chance of saying that "**other people**" are the biggest help to your creativity. That is how about half of the people in my workshops finish this sentence. The others say: time; challenge; adventurous work; freedom; being alone; rewards, etc.

In other words, **half** have good relationships with other people and can work creatively with them.

That's another reason to learn the creativity skills in this book. If you work creatively with other people in **groups** (see Part 3 of this book), then you have a great opportunity to develop relationship skills that will also help you throughout your life.

FOCUS ON YOUR DAILY ENJOYMENT, NOT THE LONG-RANGE REWARDS

Research has shown that people solve problems more creatively and turn out work with more unexpected surprises, if they focus their attention on their daily enjoyment and the fun that comes from the challenge and their total immersion in their creative work.

For high levels of creative output, you need to see the novelty in your work, enjoy your competence and self-direction, and feel that you engage in play, rather than work.

To achieve your creative potential, you need to have a sense that you work for your own satisfaction on a self-discovered problem in which you have considerable choices, especially in how to accomplish goals.

In addition, for creative thinking to flourish, you need to feel a lot of curiosity and interest, as well as have a high stability to cushion taking risks.

These conditions do not usually exist, and most students wait for the classroom or college to provide the ideal conditions that never appear. Stop it. Do not wait. Immunize yourself now against the spoilers of your creative thinking.

Immunize yourself against distractions, the external reward and punishment systems, evaluation and time pressures, competition with others, high control by others, and restricted choices.

Keep your focus on your daily enjoyment, the challenge, and your sense of competence about your work. Nurture the creative flame within you by focusing your attention on these inner motivators. Do it now.

We all want rewards: grades, honors, elected office, and the like. We have to achieve goals, meet deadlines, get positive evaluations, and obtain the approval of others. Indeed, most of us constantly work for someone else's satisfaction.

Yet, these outside rewards spoil daily creative output by over-whelming **inner motivation**: the daily enjoyment, challenge, and self-satisfaction. Help your creative thinking by focusing your attention on inner motivators. Become as self-directed as your work allows and watch your creative output and innovation soar.

Allow the enjoyment of creative thinking to motivate you.

First, you can increase enjoyment and satisfaction by staying creative as a problem solver.

Second, the sheer enjoyment of creative thinking provides a personal reason to stay creative. Creative thinking provides its own enjoyable rewards.

Stop allowing others to distract your attention with long-range **external motivators** like grades, honors, elected office, promised rewards. Of course, you want these long-range rewards. Still, focus your daily work on your inner motivators, the instant enjoyment and fun inherent in creative thinking.

Focusing your attention on money and similar rewards spoils creative effort.

A HABIT THAT SPOILS CREATIVE THINKING: We allow long-range rewards to distract us from inner motivators, our good feelings and the immediate enjoyment as we create. We allow external motivators to overpower and destroy inner motivation.

Summary: Reasons to be creative

-- To get you out of your ruts.
-- To increase your enjoyment of life.
-- To raise your fun level.
-- To better your relationships.
-- To solve problems more creatively and more effectively.
-- To increase the probability that you will succeed in your
college endeavors and achieve your goals in college and in life.

• CHAPTER 3 •
CREATIVE THINKING:
INHERITED OR LEARNED

If it isn't inherited,
where do creative thinking skills come from?

I trained as a geneticist, and the question "Is creative thinking inherited?" always intrigues me. After all, if we inherit creative thinking like I.Q., then we can do little to help anyone.

Some creative thinking skills needed at work include the following abilities. Do we inherit them?

- The ability to keep an open mind, switch tracks, see new perspectives, shift paradigms, and generate different mind sets.
- The ability to associate remote stimuli in the environment with elements in the mind and combine them into unexpected new and unusual ideas.
- The ability to generate many ideas.
- The ability to use many different problem-solving approaches.
- The ability to generate a variety of really different ideas.
- The ability to develop ideas.
- The ability to generate infrequent and uncommon ideas.
- The ability to hang in there when going against consensus and being persistent in the face of criticism.

To me, few of these skills seem inherited, and most seem learnable with appropriate training. Indeed, research comparing the scores of identical and fraternal twins on tests of these skills show that differences in creative thinking skills between people does not have a large genetic contribution. You can find the evidence in the research articles listed at the end of this chapter.

Good news. If we inherited our creative thinking skills, this book would end now with condolences. Sorry, you will always have what you have now, and training will not help. Instead, most students with reasonable mental ability become more creative after they learn to use creativity triggers.

Thus, escape from a major myth that most differences in creative thinking have a large inherited component. This myth leads to a harmful self-fulfilling prophecy: nothing can harm a high-creative person and nothing can help a low-creative person. Not so on both accounts.

First, as shown by the research on identical and fraternal twins, we do not inherit most creative thinking skills.

Second, we can learn to use creativity triggers.

Third, the environment and other external factors can help or harm creativity and creative effort.

Finally, success as a creative person also depends on other talents and abilities (inherited or otherwise), your motivation, and your interpersonal skills. The quality of your relationships, especially with your boss, affects your creative output and commitment to creative effort.

A HABIT THAT SPOILS CREATIVE THINKING: Thinking you lack creative skills. This negative put-down of yourself spoils your attempts to achieve creative outcomes. Instead, use advanced creativity triggers.

RESEARCH THAT SHOWS WE DO NOT INHERIT CREATIVE THINKING SKILLS

I suggest you skip these references. The details make my eyelids curl. However, if you must, then please be my guest...

Richmond, B.G. (1966) Creative thinking in monozygotic and dizygotic twins. Research Report from EDRS (ERIC Document Reproduction Services of the U.S. Dept. of Health, Education, and Welfare, National Institutes of Education).

Torrance, E.P. (1976) The creative child in the family; each one is "special." The Creative Child And Adult Quarterly, Winter, 195-199.

Pezzullo, T.R. (1970) The genetic components of verbal divergent thinking and short-term memory. Ph.D. Thesis, Boston College. 92 pages.

Pezzullo, T.R., E.E. Thorsen, and G.F. Madons (1972) The Heritability of Jensen's Level I and II and Divergent Thinking. Amer. Educ. Res. Jour. 9: 539-546.

Reznikoff, M., G. Domino, C. Bridges, and M. Hoffman (1973) Creative abilities in identical and fraternal twins. Behavior Genetics 3: 365-377.

Domino, G., J. Walsh, and M. Reznikoff (1976) A factor analysis of creative thinking in fraternal and identical twins. Journal Genetic Psychology 94: 211-221.

• CHAPTER 4 •
THE IMPORTANCE OF BEING
NON-EVALUATIVE

BRAINSTORMING & BRAINWRITING, TWO CREATIVITY TRIGGERS TO JUMP START IDEA-GENERATION

Unblock Your Writing And Idea-Generating Blocks ...

Rapid evaluation of new ideas depends on old information stored in your mind. New ideas can hardly survive this quick gauntlet. The petals of a new idea wither in the face of such analysis.

In this chapter, we will discuss **two** basic and important creativity triggers to stop your quick automatic NO and to help you remain non-evaluative.

Brainstorming (Non-Evaluative Listing)

During group brainstorming, a recorder writes all ideas on a note pad or flip chart paper for all to see while everyone does not evaluate. It generally produces many ideas.

Effective outcomes during brainstorming depend on everyone remaining non-evaluative. Evaluation forms from old information. When we evaluate, we immerse ourselves in old paradigms.

To escape from old perspectives, stay non-evaluative. I stress this point by calling the process 'Non-Evaluative Listing' and suggest the following guidelines:

- List **all** ideas.
- Do not think about items.
- Do not evaluate.
- Ignore repetition. Write the idea down again.
- Write bizarre ideas.
- Defer judgment and postpone evaluation until later.
- Keep the process moving.
- Do not hesitate.

Additional important recorder roles include:
- Reminds the group to stick to non-evaluative listing.
- Keeps loud members from dominating the group.
- Encourages quiet members.
- Does not discuss ideas.
- Writes bizarre ideas.
- Plays subdued leadership roles.
- Acts as a 'servant' to the creative thinking group.

The opposite of non-evaluative listing encompasses the 'gauntlet,' when you internally filter your own idea. Even if you use the gauntlet only 10% of the time, it results in 100% gauntlet. In other words, even if you only evaluate one idea out of ten, you will suppress many ideas.

A HABIT THAT SPOILS CREATIVITY: The **gauntlet**. You need total non-evaluation when listing ideas.

We shall return to non-evaluative listing, a basic building block of many idea-generating triggers later in this book. Meanwhile, enjoy an analogous approach, 'brainwriting,' for students who work alone.

Brainwriting (Non-Evaluative Automatic Writing)

Non-evaluative 'automatic writing' provides another antidote to an excessively quick negative mind. I learned it from William Drath at The Center For Creative Leadership.

To fully understand it, write a short essay on one of the following topics:

"What I did on my last vacation"
or
"What I plan to do on my next vacation."

Write your choice here...

Before you start writing, please plan carefully in your mind what you want to say. Compose a well-written essay with correct grammar, full sentences, and appropriate paragraphing.

In my creative thinking workshop, I would indicate that I may ask you to read your essay aloud. In other words, write a clear, orderly exposition.

Start now. Stop after three minutes, so please time yourself carefully. Finish writing on another sheet of paper, if necessary.

PLEASE DO NOT TURN THE PAGE AND READ FURTHER UNTIL YOU HAVE WRITTEN FOR THREE MINUTES.

Now write a short essay about the topic you did NOT choose. This time do not plan any ideas ahead of time. Write while you think quickly.

Forget correct grammar. No complete sentences. Incomplete phrases will do. No paragraphing. Do not evaluate what you write. Let your thoughts flow directly to the paper through your pen or pencil. Do not stop writing. If you stop writing, you are probably evaluating your thoughts.

When you have no thoughts, write something anyway. If necessary, write **"I have something to write"** repeatedly until your thoughts start flowing. Do not let your pen or pencil stop writing. Best of all, no one will ask you to read your essay aloud.

Start now and please stop at the end of three minutes. Finish writing on another sheet of paper, if necessary.

PLEASE DO NOT TURN THE PAGE AND READ FURTHER UNTIL YOU HAVE WRITTEN FOR THREE MINUTES.

Count the words and ideas you wrote in each essay.

If you are like most people in my workshops, you will have more words and more ideas in the second essay than the first. Freeing you from evaluation and quick negative criticism short-circuits your habitual automatic No, improves the creative atmosphere in your mind, and helps you produce more creative outcomes.

Some guidelines for automatic writing follow:

- Write all thoughts.
- Do not hold back. Let it flow!
- Orderly thoughts not required.
- Correct grammar unimportant.
- Incomplete phrases fine.
- Complete sentences not necessary.
- Paragraphing not important.
- Do not evaluate.
- Bypass your hand. Be the paper. Let your thoughts flow directly to the paper.
- What you write does not have to fit the topic. That boxes you in and you measure every thought against the topic.
- If you do not write, assume you evaluate. Write: "I do have something to write" until you have something to write, and then write, write, write...

I use automatic writing, a valuable creativity trigger, to overcome obstacles to my creative thinking or my writing. It usually cures my writer's block.

And I use it and non-evaluative listing to unblock my idea-generating blocks. It allows interesting ideas to emerge and installs a creative atmosphere in your mind to help you make remote connections to shift paradigms and solve problems creatively.

Advanced Automatic Writing

Practice an advanced version of automatic writing by placing two writing tablets next to each other. On one tablet, write automatically as described above. On the other tablet, write "I have something to write" when you find yourself blocked. To help overcome the block, switch from one tablet to other as the spirit moves you.

Another approach: As they come to you, write your ideas on 3" x 5" index cards, one idea per card (See 'Idea Card' in Chapter 13). When finished, sort the cards in the order you want. Use these cards as an outline to help you write automatically on the two writing tablets as described above, except now use one tablet for the finished writing you want and switch to the other tablet for random thoughts when you find yourself blocked.

The important thing: keep your hand writing automatically. Merge with the paper as you write. Become the paper and pen.

A TRUE STORY: I wrote the first draft of this book, and many subsequent added sections, using automatic writing.

Being non-evaluative is essential to creativity.

• CHAPTER 5 •
BIZARRE IDEAS AS
CREATIVITY TRIGGERS

You Want To Be More Creative, Don't You?

BIZARRE TRIGGER-IDEAS SHIFT PARADIGMS AND SPARK BETTER IDEAS

Creative thinking yields many non-useful, even bizarre, ideas. However, all ideas, even bizarre ideas, can act as useful stepping stones to provoke better ideas, and to even shift paradigms.

For example, consider the statement: "Let's train bears to climb telephone poles in winter and shake off the ice that breaks the transmission wires." One person proposed this idea in a spirit of fun to prevent ice from breaking power lines in a mountainous region where winters are cold and rainy. Someone in the meeting had complained about being harassed by bears on one repair trip. This led one of the people, in a spirit of fun, to suggest training bears to climb the poles and shake the ice loose, clearly a bizarre idea.

A second person, again in jest, suggested putting pots of honey on the top of the poles so the bears would climb the poles and shake the ice off the wires, another bizarre idea.

A third person suggested, still in fun, using helicopters to place the pots of honey on the poles to attract the bears, also a bizarre idea.

Yet this led to a solution worth testing. The down draft from helicopters flying over the wires might knock the ice off. ***

*** For another telling of this tale, see "The Honey Pot: A Lesson in Creativity & Diversity" by Elaine Camper, April 2, 1993, at: http://www.insulators.info/articles/ppl.htm

And also here: "Re-engineering Tool Kit: 15 Tools and Technologies for Re-engineering Your Organization" by Cheryl Currid, Prima Publishing, 1996.

People embellish this story with each retelling. Still, it illustrates that bizarre trigger-ideas spark useful solutions. Unless you encourage and help bizarre ideas to survive, you will hinder creative thinking and lose opportunities for creativity.

A HABIT THAT SPOILS CREATIVE THINKING: We squelch bizarre trigger-ideas instead of using them to shift paradigms and spark better ideas.

LINEAR AND NONLINEAR CREATIVE THINKING

Many ways to get new and useful ideas exist. One way uses **linear** creative thinking. We use this most because of its low risk. It flows like this...

A => B => C => D => New And Useful Idea.

You check each rung carefully for truth and logic before moving to the next. You know your direction, how to get there, when you get there, and why you wanted to get there in the first place. Very precise, analytical, and certain.

Does it work? Of course. We base most of our rational thinking on this model. We constructed much of our civilization using this approach.

Another way to get new and useful ideas uses **nonlinear** thinking. Ideas leap about.

$$X \Rightarrow L \Rightarrow Z \Rightarrow R \Rightarrow E \Rightarrow Y \dots$$

and eventually, out of bizarre trigger-ideas and very remote connections, a paradigm shift occurs, and some new and useful ideas emerge.

A very uncertain process. You do not know the direction, how you will get there, when you get there, or why you wanted to arrive there. Risky, unpredictable, and ambiguous, it often leads nowhere. However, when a new and useful idea emerges, it likely represents a paradigm shift, unique & original.

Look at the fun nonlinear creative thinking path that turned the bears and the pots of honey into the helicopters.

Repair man reports harassment by bears.

↓

Train bears to climb poles and shake ice off wires.

↓

Place pots of honey on top of poles to attract bears to climb.

↓

Use helicopters to place pots of honey on top of poles to attract bears.

↓

Use the down blast of helicopters to shake ice off the wires.

None of these bizarre ideas logically led to the other, yet they all led to a possible useful outcome. Had the chairperson or anyone else at the meeting stopped the process or insisted on seriousness, the paradigm shift and the useful innovation would not have occurred.

A HABIT THAT SPOILS CREATIVE THINKING: We don't deliberately misperceive the world to obtain a **nonlinear** viewpoint and a paradigm shift.

Many creativity triggers described in this book depend on students allowing bizarre trigger-ideas to flourish and eventually spark unique and sensible solutions to problems. Bizarre trigger-ideas form a creative foundation for idea-generation.

• PART 2 •
THE CREATIVE ATMOSPHERE

• CHAPTER 6 •
CREATE A CREATIVE ATMOSPHERE
IN YOUR MIND

A TRUE STORY: I have a friend who uses his constant, gentle wit and says funny things. His humor helps when the discussion becomes overly serious. "Everyone thinks I'm humorous," he once said. "Actually, I'm out of control." Indeed, he acts very spontaneously.

A HABIT THAT SPOILS CREATIVE THINKING: We inhibit our spontaneity and repress our wit and humor.

The Creative Atmosphere In Your Mind

The creative climate in your mind has profound effects on your creative output. Your paradigms, beliefs and thoughts propel your behavior and your thinking into creative or not-so-creative activities. For example, if you believe you can't think creatively, then you won't. And what's worse, you won't make the effort to learn how.

Here's another. If you believe in certain assumed boundaries and unwarranted assumptions, or adhere to certain unstated criteria and an unrealistic sense of fairness in your mind, then your belief system and paradigms will keep you stuck and spoil your creative thinking.

And here's a crushing example. If you have a highly developed habitual automatic No and a fondness for quick negative criticism, not only will you spoil everyone else's creative thinking, you will also cut down on your own creative output. Your creative thinking will be mired in excessive gloom and prophecies of failure, even though you can think very creatively, pulling negative comments out of the blue.

When solving problems, instead of shifting the paradigm and striking out into new territory, our mind focuses on a previously successful solution, and we continue the old timeworn ways of doing things, even if counter productive. This dampens the creative atmosphere in your mind.

The antidote to this habit starts with becoming aware of this process and taking measures to reduce or eliminate it. That's one purpose of Part 2 of this book.

Let us start with some fun puzzles to discover how we spoil creative thinking in ourselves and others, and the antidote to such spoiler-habits.

IX, A FUN EXERCISE

Each of us has far more creative thinking ability than we suspect. A bit of fun will show you how.

Add one line to a "IX" and turn it into a six. Spend about three to four minutes on this problem before moving on. No peeking at the answers yet, please.

There are many solutions. The most common: add an "S" to the "IX" and produce a ... SIX. If you got this, congratulations.

If you did not get this answer, why not? Like many students in my creative thinking workshop, one or more of the following may have blocked you:

- You forgot that words can express numbers.
- You looked for a straight line. You forgot that lines also curve.
- You connected this in your mind with a match stick problem.
- You got stuck on Roman numerals.

Our thoughts act like they get trapped by ruts in our minds and cannot get out. These ruts are called paradigms, old beliefs, and thought patterns. And out of habit, we keep trying to find a solution

within these ruts even though they do not work to solve the new problem.
lem.

Mind Ruts

These mind-ruts, collectors of thoughts, capture problems and send them down the same old paths. Once you get stuck in a mind-rut, you find it hard to get out without deliberate creative thinking, that is, without using creativity triggers.

Every time a related new problem arises, you return to the old mind-ruts that succeeded before. If you stuff a new problem into an old mind rut that once worked, you generate the same timeworn solution.

Since a mind-rut gets more entrenched each time you use it to solve a problem, you eventually no longer look for new ways to perceive and deal with a new problem. The problem drops into that 'huge' mind-rut and you exert your thinking efforts to push the problem toward an adequate solution, a quick fix, instead of seeking alternatives. You need to shift paradigms using creativity triggers to get out of old mind-ruts.

Thus, to convert "IX" to "SIX" you need to get out of at least two mind ruts and into new paradigms: one that tells you "words can express numbers," and another that tells you "lines can curve." If you don't do that, you will not get to "SIX" from "IX."

Programmed Mind Ruts

To demonstrate mind-ruts in my workshop, I ask about favorite colors. About 50% of the attendees say their favorite color is red, the rest say blue. How can this be? With many hundreds of colors from which to choose, almost all say red or blue. What happened to orange, purple, or blonde?

Another example: about half of the attendees say their favorite fruit is an apple, the other half say banana. Again, how can this be? With the many dozens of fruits available, almost all say apple or banana. I'm told that in Mexico they say mango and papaya. In New Zealand they say the kiwi.

Mind-ruts are programs instilled in us by experience, training, schooling, and whatever. To be creative, we need to free our minds and get rid of non-useful mind-ruts, programming, paradigms, perspectives, or whatever you call it, That's partly what this book is about.

Fortunately, we can decide what to get rid of and what to retain. You control your choice.

A HABIT THAT SPOILS CREATIVE THINKING: We allow our thoughts to get stuck in an old established mind-rut, and we stay stuck in old paradigms. We do not deliberately search out alternative mind-ruts or shift paradigms using appropriate creativity triggers.

You might have shifted the paradigm and gotten into other perspectives, and other answers, such as:

- Add a 6, and make 1X 6 (one times six). This equals 6.

- Cover the top half of the IX with a thick line, and turn it upside down so it looks like this: vi

- Move the vertical line in IX to the right and one slanting line of the X to the left to produce a distorted \/ |

- Fold the paper through the middle of the IX, and turn it over so all you see is vi

These last two solutions may disturb you because I did not add a line. Try to discover what mind-rut(s) grabbed your thoughts. Perhaps the following:

- Fairness: I said add a line, and it seems unfair not to add one.
- Making Unwarranted Assumptions: You might have assumed the added line must attach to the answer.

Actually, I did not specify where or when you add the line, perhaps on the next page, or in the next edition of this book, or you could add it next week. If it disturbs you that much, please add a line just below the solution like this: <u>VI</u>

A HABIT THAT SPOILS CREATIVE THINKING: Solutions to problems have to seem fair, fit preconceived notions, old paradigms, and unstated phantom criteria that no longer apply.

A HABIT THAT SPOILS CREATIVE THINKING: We make unwarranted assumptions about problems and do not check them out. We stay stuck in old paradigms and old mind-ruts.

You trigger your mind-ruts and paradigms by words, remote connections, visual impressions, ideas, etc. They keep you glued to the past. Connecting new problems with old mind ruts and paradigms produces the same timeworn solutions and spoils creative thinking, the closed mind syndrome.

You easily get locked into an old, ineffectual mind-rut or paradigm, because you maintain it with old ideas and traditions, not by current success. To avoid this, shift into new paradigms.

A HABIT THAT SPOILS CREATIVE THINKING: The quick fix depends on accepting the first adequate solution to a problem, thereby denying your creative ability to find a better solution.

To avoid the quick fix, set a quota for three to five different ideas before choosing a solution (10 different ideas are better). Or non-evaluatively list all the ideas you can think of in a three-minute brainstorming session.

A HABIT THAT SPOILS CREATIVE THINKING: One habit based on the quick fix includes rushing to generate solutions before carefully analyzing the problem (or examining alternative paradigms) to make sure you work on the right problem. You use old paradigms instead of new ones.

Old paradigms distort current reality and produce an inability to even see other alternatives. They lead to low quality solutions if you use the wrong paradigms. Since they become more established each time they successfully solve a problem, they diverge from reality as time passes. We refer to successful paradigms as 'perspectives,' while we refer to unsuccessful paradigms as 'ruts.'

A HABIT THAT SPOILS CREATIVE THINKING: We do not search a single paradigm for the entire range of possible new ideas.

A HABIT THAT SPOILS CREATIVE THINKING: We do not explore new ideas for additional paradigms.

Later in this book, we will use advanced creativity triggers to alter these habits, get into different perspectives, and shift to new paradigms by analyzing problems and listing many 'How-to' problem statements. We will then use idea-generating triggers, and other creativity triggers to select and combine ideas into trigger-proposals, and then into quality solutions.

PARADIGMS AND "HALF OF EIGHT," ANOTHER FUN EXERCISE

How many ways do you think you can represent "half of eight?"
Write down the number here (   ).
Now list all the ways you can think of to represent "half of eight."
Spend at least five to ten minutes before you move on.

Students in my creative thinking workshops have represented "half of eight" in the following ways:

● Mathematical Solutions

(1 x 4), (2 x 2), (3 x 1.25), (4 x 1), etc.

(2^2), (square root of 16), (2 times the square root of 4), (4 times the square root of 1), etc.

(1+3), (2+2, (3+1, (5-1), (6-2), etc.

(8 divided by 2), (12 divided by 3), (16 divided by 4), etc.

● Solutions That Slice "8" In Half

Slice the 8 horizontally in half to produce o and o, which are the top and bottom halves of 8.

Slice the 8 vertically into the left and right halves of 8.

Halve the 8 in all directions leading to an infinity of distorted answers. Indeed, you might halve all diagrams of eight in all directions, including eight, VIII, 4+4, and other representations of eight.

● Solutions That Write "Four" In Different Ways

4; four; IV; IIII; etc.

Ideographs that write 'four' in Chinese, Japanese, Sanskrit, Arabic, Hindu, ancient Egyptian, etc.

• Solutions Using Codes For "Four

100 (represents 4 in binary numbers); 11 (represents 4 in ternary numbers), etc.

Morse or semaphore code.

Deaf sign language.

Boat pennant representing four.

Sign of Four (see the Sherlock Holmes story).

500 (1000 is the binary number for 8; one-half of this is 500); also 10 and 00 (cutting 1000 in half vertically).

• Other Solutions

Show four fingers (what a four-year old does when asked his or her age).

7:30 (the German, halb acht).

Hit the ground four times with his hoof (what Clever Hans, the horse, did).

The telephone company has a special frequency for 'four' that represents "half of eight" in sound).

Braille (for the blind).

Now imagine you sit in my workshop, and you only hear me say: "List all the ways to represent half of 8." I do not write it, just say it. Would you get into the following perspective: half of ATE. If you did, how would you use it? Would you halve 'ATE' in all directions. Would you write: "hungry" or draw a half eaten apple or an apple pie cut into 4 pieces?

Learn From "Half Of Eight/Ate"

You can learn a lot from half of eight/ate.

First: Numerous and diverse perspectives exist for all problems, even one as seemingly simple as half of eight, and certainly for many serious problems we take for granted. This constitutes the quick fix, ignoring rich possibilities. You say you don't have time, another deterrent to creative thinking.

A HABIT THAT SPOILS CREATIVE THINKING: We do not spend enough time shifting paradigms. You do not allot enough time to explore different perspectives, to analyze problems relentlessly, and to avoid the quick fix.

Second: In my creative thinking workshop, we suggest many solutions to the "half of 8" problem; yet each person discovers only a few. Thus, one of the reasons to solve problems in groups includes the sharing of perspectives to shift paradigms. Each person has unique knowledge and experience. Therefore, his or her perspectives provide unique and valuable viewpoints. Later, we will examine creativity triggers to ensure effective sharing of paradigms and perspectives in groups.

Third: Do not rush when solving problems. A hasty, early choice cuts down on better possibilities. Creative thinking takes time and often means communicating with other students to discover new perspectives and paradigms.

If you desire, check out Appendix II, more creativity-spoiling habits using an old reliable puzzle: 'Nine Magic Dots.'

• CHAPTER 7 •
THE CREATIVE CLIMATE:
HELP OTHERS SHARE THEIR IDEAS
WITH YOU

A TRUE STORY: At one workshop, a manager told me he had learned creativity triggers like brainstorming before, but never the habits that affect the creative climate with clarity. He claimed a positive atmosphere was missing, and that negative habits spoiled creative thinking all the time. As he said: "Creativity triggers by themselves are not enough. A creative atmosphere is essential."

Quick Negative Criticism

In my workshops, some people (about 3%) state that they feel frustrated, even angry, when they are creative (not a good feeling), because of the quick negative comments of other people. What a shame to miss out on the joy of creativity.

When presented with a new idea most students make a negative comment under the guise of honest criticism, devil's advocate, or constructive criticism. Indeed, quick negative criticism inflicts our society. "You don't want me to lie, they say.

A HABIT THAT SPOILS CREATIVE THINKING: We respond to new ideas with quick negative criticism and an habitual automatic NO that usually maims or kills new ideas, and spoils creative thinking.

Yet criticism spoils creative thinking. Only the toughest risk takers will volunteer to share the first-stage, half-baked ideas that most of us have. Successful creative people, who have written about their creative thinking, agree that quick negative criticism has a devastating effect on new ideas. Albert Einstein made this point in his autobiography.

Of all the ways to spoil creative thinking during problem solving, quick negative criticism heads the list. Still, you have to give honest opinions about new ideas. Some ways to do this without spoiling creative thinking and stifling student's desire to present new ideas follow:

Suppose a student brings you an idea he likes very much. How should you respond? Very carefully, I hope.

First, you should be thinking that whatever the idea's flaws, you need to trust this student. Consider that the new idea has merit. After all, its proposer thinks so.

Second, you do not want to discourage this person and other students from bringing you ideas and proposals in the future. Indeed, you want to encourage idea-sharing.

Third, you do not want this student to leave feeling resentful because you rejected his/her idea.

Finally, you want this student to tell you about their idea without feeling defensive, or under pressure. Change the hot seat into a positive creative climate.

Given all this, you do not say: "That's a lousy idea."

IDEA-HELPING PROCESSES THAT INVITE IDEA-SHARING

How can you help the submission of new ideas? In my creative thinking workshop I recommend the following:

I.P.N.C. (Interest, Positive, Negative, Concerns)

I.P.N.C. Is a bit over-structured, but by learning to use it, you focus your attitude in the right direction.

When using 'I.P.N.C.,' your initial comments indicate your **Interest (I)** in the idea, and in what the proposer thinks about it, followed by all the **Positive (P)** comments you can muster. Then state your

Negative (N) comments as concerns. Finally, your comments indicate **Curiosity (C)** about the idea, and ask how you can help the person address with your concerns.

Note that I.P.N.C. surrounds your negative comments with help and encouragement, with an invitation to discuss the idea further now, and to hear new ideas in the future. Avoid sarcastic, jeering comments.

Let's see how I.P.N.C might work. What do you say when someone presents a new idea they like? Use I.P.N.C. to open the discussion.
- **I**nterest: That's a very interesting idea.
- **P**ositive: I like it because it ...
- **N**egative: I am a little concerned that...
- **C**uriosity: I wonder why you like it? How will you use it?
How can I help?"

Notice that you have pointed out what you think is a fatal flaw in a way that helps the other person feel encouraged. Students often ask why not start with direct questions. In my experience, and from what others tell me, many students perceive immediate, quick questioning as a negative response that puts them on the defensive, and lowers their willingness to propose new ideas again.

The student with the idea can now respond to your I.P.N.C. comments in several ways. He or she might say: "You're right. I had not noticed that. Thanks for telling me. I'll change the concept," and leave, hopefully feeling encouraged, and at least thinking you took his or her ideas seriously. On the other hand, they might explain how their idea has merits you did not detect.

Now aren't you glad you didn't say "That's a lousy idea" when you first saw it? Of course, it might have been easier if the other person had made it clearer. This leads us to another habit that spoils creative thinking.

A HABIT THAT SPOILS CREATIVE THINKING: We expect sellers of ideas to present their ideas in perfect form. No half-baked, half-developed ideas for us. Every "i" dotted, every "t" crossed, every concept clear, every label and term used correctly, with no errors of spelling or grammar.

In other words, we expect them to help us before we help their idea. Beware. Creative ideas rarely appear in perfect form, and negative consequences occur if you insist on this. Students will expend valuable time and effort toward perfection. Besides, few of us have training in selling ideas anyway.

Yes-If

Yes-if is a less structured and more relaxed than I.P.N.C. And you will find it easier to use. Curb your automatic NO, say "Yes, if...," and then describe the conditions needed to get from NO to a conditional YES. Watch the climate change from a negative one that deters creative thinking to a positive, idea-helping climate.

A TRUE STORY: At the end of one creative thinking workshop, a participant who tried "yes-if" for the first time confirmed its effectiveness.

He said he noticed that "yes-if" not only kept him away from his automatic No, but led him to listen to the new ideas presented to him very intently to discover the ways to convert a NO to a conditional YES.

As he put it: "Yes-if converted me into a collaborator to help a new idea get going, rather than a judge."

A TRUE STORY: A participant wrote me after a workshop and said: "Yes-if turned me into a better listener, one who is more empathetic, better understood, and now more predictable. My effectiveness improved by leaps and bounds!"

Let's see how you might use Yes-if.

Say "**YES**," there are many interesting and useful features about this idea, "**IF**, we can improve this snag..."

Clear, supportive, and crisp. Very useful when hearing ideas on the run.

What's Good About It

If none of these approaches seem comfortable, you might use "What's Good About It" and state three positive statements first.

Pretend Your Boss Presented The Idea

Or, you could pretend your department chair presents any idea you hear, and devise your own idea-helping approach. Your attitude counts a great deal when you help ideas. Increased idea sharing and better idea improvement will result.

Other statements to encourage new ideas include:
• The value of that idea is....
• That seems like a useful idea. Can we build on it?
• A good start. How can we help it?
• It seems you are getting somewhere.
• Describe that in more detail. Tell me more about it.
• How can we make this work?
• I would be interested in what you have to say.
• Tell me what you are thinking.
• I like your idea. How we can get over this difficulty.
• That idea has value. Let's get the bugs out.
• You may well be right. Still, let us look at it another way.

Quick Spoilers Of Creative Thinking

The more polite alternatives to I.P.N.C. and Yes-if include the following quick idea spoilers.

• It's already been proposed.
• We've never done it that way before... or We tried that before.

- If it ain't broke, why fix it.
- Once you analyze the problem properly, the solution seems obvious (so we don't need to generate more ideas).
- We don't need any more new ideas around here. What we need are more doers, implementers, idea champions, etc.
- The problem with that idea is...
- It's not in the budget …
- We haven't the personnel.
- What will they think?
- We would have suggested it before if it were any good.
- We're too small for that ... or We're too big for that.
- We have too many ideas already.
- It has been the same for a long time; so, it must be good.
- I just know it won't work.
- That's not our problem.
- You'll never sell that to the administration.
- Why something new now?

Stop using these quick spoilers. They have many detrimental effects.

First, many students suppress and stop expressing their ideas.

Second, creative students stop being creative in school.

Third, some students become defensive and apologetic, and shoot-down their own ideas before anyone else does.

Finally, some students tend to do things the same old safe, complacent way instead of taking risks, shifting paradigms, and turning half-baked, half-developed, bizarre ideas into winners.

Not all new ideas pan out, of course; but unless you deliberately and relentlessly help develop new ideas, they perish, and complacency takes over.

I do not remember who said it, but if you want to be around butterflies, you have to generously help many caterpillars. Help new ideas with I.P.N.C. And Yes-if. Or pretend every idea you hear comes from your department chair.

ASSERT THAT YOU WANT OTHERS TO HELP YOUR IDEA

When a group quickly shoots down ideas, many students get defensive and start shooting down their own ideas first, that is, if they actually muster up the courage to share them. Some ways they do it include:

• This may not work, but...
• You'll probably laugh, but...
• It might be a dead end, but...
• I'm no genius, but...

Stop shooting down your own ideas with such apologetic phrases. Instead, assert that you want others to help you develop your new idea further. Take responsibility. Change the creative climate around you.

A HABIT THAT SPOILS CREATIVE THINKING: We don't object when other people (students, faculty, classmates, colleagues, family, friends) stifle our ideas.

We allow other people to shoot down our ideas and spoil our creative thinking., and we do the same to our own ideas.

Stop doing this. Take responsibility for the creative atmosphere around you.

TAKE RESPONSIBILITY FOR THE CREATIVE CLIMATE

How responsible are you for the creative thinking of others? A lot? A little? Not at all? Actually 100%.

Why 100% responsible? Because you can stop saying "NO" so easily. Your automatic No devastates the creative thinking of others. Also because you can use I.P.N.C., Yes-If, and other idea-helping skills to create a creative climate for others. Pretend all the ideas you hear come from your department chair.

Once again, how responsible are you for your own creative thinking? A little? A lot? Actually 100%.

Why? Because you can assert to others who have a large automatic No and quick negative criticism. Ask them to help you develop your idea, not kill it. Be assertive and create a creative climate around you.

Help creative thinking by squelching criticism, not new ideas. A new idea is like a brown, ugly seed. You do not know whether it will grow into a lovely flower or a common weed until you plant it and nurture it. Likewise, a newly formed idea is half-developed or half-baked; what you call it depends on whether it is your idea, and on whether you like it.

Students find new ideas disconcerting. They do not know the direction the idea will take or whether it will get there. Many mistakes will occur. Surrounded by high risk, no one can predict the future and prove in advance any new idea will succeed. Because students find new ideas unpredictable and hard to develop, students find them easy to reject. Hence the quick automatic NO.

In summary, accept 100% responsibility for the creative climate around you. You can use I.P.N.C. and Yes-If to help the ideas of other students. You can assert to help yourself. You can change a negative climate to a positive one by your own actions!

A HABIT THAT SPOILS CREATIVE THINKING: We discourage & squelch new ideas, especially bizarre ideas.

Summary: Foster The Creative Climate
In Your Life

By creative climate, I mean the attitudes and behaviors that lead to the freer use of everyone's ideas during problem solving. This includes the use of 'helping and reinforcing' responses to new ideas, willingness to examine and explore different points of view, and deliberate searching for new connections between facts, beliefs, and ideas to create quality solutions.

You can foster such a positive climate by looking for the good in ideas before concentrating on what is bad, using I.P.N.C., Yes-If, and other approaches. You can stimulate others to do likewise by eagerly listening to new ideas and find ing whatever is good and useful in them. You can eliminate the times you and others take automatic pot shots at each other's ideas.

The quick automatic NO impedes a creative climate for solving problems. You can help encourage positive climate factors by setting the example, the tone, and the mood for everyone else.   A positive creative climate is a rarity rather than commonplace. So, it takes much courage and patience to stay creative and to express new ideas. And it takes courage and patience to help another person with their idea rather than voice your quick negative criticism. It takes courage and patience to defer judgement of ideas during problem solving meetings.

You can become the prime mover toward a positive creative climate. You need to stay optimistic. You need to convince others by modeling the behaviors you want to encourage. You need to understand the great disadvantages of the quick automatic NO response, and you must help the what's-good-about-it approach until it becomes the habitual response of other students around you.

Remember: Creative thinking support leads to **MORE** creative thinking support. Lack of creative thinking support leads to more **LACK** of creative thinking support.

• CHAPTER 8 •
CLIMB THE PROBLEM-SOLVING LADDER: WATCH FOR THE THREE KEY CREATIVE RUNGS

I hesitate to do it now, but sometimes the "S" word (serious) intrudes and spoils frolicking fun. You must solve your "S" problems seriously. To start, imagine a ladder with eight rungs. To solve your problem creatively, you must climb the problem-solving ladder.

Note: *** indicates the 3 key creative rungs on the ladder.

*** Rung #1. Analyze the problem.

Rung #2. Establish the criteria so you can select the real problem statement(s).

Rung #3. Select problem statement(s) you want to solve.

*** Rung #4. List many ideas.
*** Rung #5. Combine ideas into creative trigger-proposals.

Rung #6. Identify the criteria to select quality solutions.

Rung #7. Convert trigger-proposals into quality solutions that meet the criteria.

Rung #8. Make action plans to implement a quality solution.

NOTE: *** indicates the 3 key creative rungs on the ladder.

This sequence incorporates some important concepts essential to shift paradigms and produce high quality solutions.

First: The three key creative rungs in problem solving …
- Rung #1: Analyze and uncover the real problem
- Rung #4: List many ideas
- Rung #5: Combine ideas into creative trigger-proposals.

Welcome bizarre and exotic trigger-ideas in each rung. Use them to spark better ideas. Stay positive throughout. Let your imagination soar. Do not discard or ridicule any idea. Instead, choose what you want to use. Keep what's left for future reference or discard them by gentle neglect.

The more bizarre you analyze a problem, the more likely your imagination will produce a paradigm shift and a practical solution that differs from past approaches. Thus:

Bizarre Problem Statements	=>	Bizarre Risky Ideas	=>	Bizarre Trigger- Proposals	=>	New and Different Workable Solutions

Second: Avoid rushing to generate solutions until you extensively analyze the problem to make sure you work on the right problem. Do not stuff the new problem into a comfortable old mind-rut or paradigm.

Students who spend more time on Rung #1 (analyzing the problem) usually produce solutions more creative than students who rush to Rung #4 (generating ideas). This makes a great deal of sense, since jolting your mind first to pursue new directions, new paradigms, and new perspectives ensures that you generate unusual ideas and solutions that focus on the real problem.

A HABIT THAT SPOILS CREATIVE THINKING: We rush to generate solutions before we adequately examine and analyze the problem, a variation of the quick fix.

Third: Do not actively reject unacceptable problem statements, ideas, or trigger-proposals. Just leave them behind as you chose others. Discarded thoughts may work later.

Fourth: Do not identify the **criteria** before Rung #6. If you do, you box in your creativity as you prematurely measure problem definitions and ideas against the criteria. Scuttle premature criteria.

Often you prematurely obtain criteria from others or remember unstated, phantom criteria from previous experiences. Deal directly with such criteria, or they will inhibit and drown your creativity. Get rid of them. Use forced-withdrawal and reverse the criteria. Here's how:

1. Non-evaluatively list all given and unstated, phantom criteria. Set a quota for at least 10 to 20 phantom criteria.

2. Reverse your criteria. Distort them. Shrink them. Magnify them. Play "what if" with them. Do whatever you can to make them insignificant.

3. Later, when you finish generating ideas and trigger-proposals (see Chapter 13), you can return to realistic criteria (Rung 6). Then select ideas and proposals that fit your criteria.

A HABIT THAT SPOILS CREATIVE THINKING: We box in our creativity by identifying criteria before we generate problem statements or ideas.

Fifth: After all that effort and fun, every solution you intend to implement deserves an action plan with detailed action steps (see Chapter 16).

Proposals without a plan perch perilously close to perishing.

• CHAPTER 9 •
RUNG #1.
SHIFT PARADIGMS AND
FIND THE REAL PROBLEM

(THE 1ST KEY CREATIVE RUNG
ON THE LADDER)

RUNG #1. SHIFT PARADIGMS AND
FIND THE REAL PROBLEM

You know many **logical** ways to unearth the real problem. Don't abandon them. In addition, analyze the problem innovatively (Rung 1 in the problem-solving sequence in Chapter 8). Talk the problem out. Think the problem through. Everything helps shift the paradigm.

Gaining new perspectives and new paradigms while unearthing the real problem creatively can happen in many ways.

Step back, take on a new identity and pretend you are someone or something else; say, a frog, an elephant, a sea gull, a shark, or a person from another culture or another profession.

Deliberately reverse and distort your view of the problem. S y s-tematically list what you like about the problem area and what you want to improve.

Answer the who, what, where, why, when, with whom, and again, why about the problem.

These approaches jolt your mind into a multitude of fresh, new perspectives that escape old paradigms. Above all, you need to list numerous diverse problem statements. I have provided specific directions and detailed creativity triggers in this chapter.

Problem statements provide the **foundation** for successful problem solving. The statement(s) you choose determine the direction of your thinking and the kind of ideas you generate.

A HABIT THAT SPOILS CREATIVE THINKING: We do not analyze problems innovatively.

We often spend time solving the wrong problem; so, the problem appears repeatedly, never effectively identified and resolved. To end this cycle, transform and modify the starting problem statement, generate a long list of diverse problem statements before idea generation. Thus, you open up a broad range of new perspectives and paradigms, a key first rung to achieving quality solutions.

Work with others, if possible. Different perceptions and paradigms will more likely surface because of the unique experiences and points of view each person brings to the process.

The problem statement will determine the kind of the ideas you generate later. So, focus on many problem statements to keep from overlooking important directions or committing to an inappropriate solution too soon. Make sure you solve the **real** problem.

What-if

Fantasy helps. The what-if creativity trigger makes you look at your problem from many different necessary perspectives, so you don't smother your creativity. Many of the creativity triggers described in this chapter follow a what-if pattern.

Turn On Your "How-to" Thinking

The "How-to" creativity trigger injects a useful, more serious note than What-if. Start your problem statements with 'How to' to keep you from getting into solutions too soon. The creativity triggers described below provide help. Spend hours, even days, listing 'How-to' problem statements, if the problem warrants it.

By listing many How-to statements, you search for new, fresh paradigms, perspectives, and unexpected views of the problem. Such statements provide a broad-based foundation on which to later generate ideas and develop solutions. Do not destroy the foundation by rushing to generate ideas. Shift the paradigm and uncover the real problem first.

A HABIT THAT SPOILS CREATIVE THINKING: We rush to generate solutions before extensively exposing the problem and establishing a good foundation on which to generate ideas.

Write your starting problem statement:
How to...

Discover your real problem by completing the following:

How to...	How to launch...	How to schedule...
How to gain...	How to switch...	How to maximize...
How to improve...	How to admire...	How to learn to...
How to change...	How to begin...	How to perform...
How to add...	How to revive...	How to flourish...
How to fix...	How to upgrade...	How to make...
How to minimize...	How to arrange...	How to end...
How to do...	How to enrich...	How to disclose...
How to enhance...	How to start...	How to restore...
How to cope with...	How to expand...	How to destroy...
How to restore...	How to amplify...	How to inspire...
How to get rid of...	How to build...	How to motivate...
How to produce...	How to manage...	How to deal with...
How to exceed...	How to verify...	How to lose...
How to reduce...	How to start...	How to conquer...
How to deliver...	How to enlarge...	How to modify...
How to handle...	How to establish...	How to challenge...
How to eliminate...	How to succeed...	How to reward...
How to change...	How to attempt...	How to satisfy...
How to develop...	How to adapt...	How to establish...
How to control...	How to originate...	How to afford...

How to increase...	How to appreciate...	How to transpose...
How to reject...	How to achieve...	How to scar...
How to persuade...	How to tell...	How to substitute...
How to enrich...	How to share...	How to rearrange...
How to provoke...	How to distribute...	How to use...
How to encourage...	How to assemble...	How to subtract...
How to invent...	How to reverse...	How to attempt....
How to create...	How to twist...	How to alter...
How to enjoy...	How to blend...	How to enjoy...
	How to combine...	How to ...

Stick with it. Your patience will be rewarded.

Analogies & Metaphors

Analogies and metaphors help you think creatively in new places.

For example, if you want to improve paint, list the characteristics and properties of paint, such as, color, aesthetics, hides dirt, protective boundary, etc. Identify other places where a protective boundary exists, list its properties, and force combinations to improve paint. Some examples follow:

• In plants: the boundary between woods and pasture depends on soil, nutrients, and cultivation. This leads to thoughts on how to make a paint that has different colors on different surfaces. In addition, fungus on the bark of trees indicates dead wood, triggering how to make paint that signals rot underneath.

• In the animal kingdom: the skin of the octopus and squid changes color with different moods, triggering thoughts on how to make a paint that will change a room's color with the occupant's mood. Also, animal skin has a protective boundary that can self-heal and self-cleanse, triggering how to make paint self-repair and self-cleanse.

• In physics: charges at boundaries repel, triggering thoughts on how to make a paint that repels dirt.

• In an artist's painting: the boundary between objects results from different colors and pigments, triggering how to make a paint that produces a picture when spread on the wall.

• A book: its covers trigger thoughts to make a paint that opens to reveal what it covers and then closes to hide, perhaps even a zipper-effect.

Recycle this procedure using another characteristic or property of paint to shift paradigms. Expect good results.

The Problem's Essence

Unfortunately, knowing a problem well means you have a myriad of old paradigms and old thoughts in your mind that spoil new thinking. To avoid these old pictures, use this version of forced-withdrawal to work on the problem indirectly at first. Start with the 'essence' of the problem, the action verb that captures the main activity.

For example, the essence (or action verb) of:
- an auto jack is lifting things;
- a wheelbarrow is transporting things;
- walking on water is floating things or freezing water;
- a bullet proof vest is impenetrability;
- reuse of cans and bottles is recycling things;
- improving the can opener is opening things;
- keeping food from spoiling is preserving things.

Therefore, a creativity team seeking to improve the can opener first discussed ways to **open** things using analogies and metaphors from industry, animals, plants, other cultures, etc. What happened? They discussed:
- When you squeeze the base of a dog's mouth, it will open
- When a clam relaxes a muscle, tension on the back hinge of the shell forces the clam open
- When peas ripen, the tough covering develops a weak seam, and the pea pod opens.

The team forced combinations between the weak seam of the pea pod and opening cans. This did not lead to an improved can opener, as they originally intended, but it did lead to opening cans by pulling a weak seam, a common way to open most cans now.

This example illustrates **nonlinear** creative thinking described in Chapter 5.

Targeted Analogies And Metaphors Based On The Problem's Essence

Combine the two previous creativity triggers into a truly exceptional approach that shifts paradigms and opens a flood of new approaches.

1. Forget about the problem statement and deal only with the **action verb** that captures the essence of the problem.

2. Generate examples of the problem's essence as metaphors and analogies from the plant and animal world; industry and government; professions; other countries; ethnic and religious groups; the historical past; exotic other-world places; the wild west; etc.

3. Choose one example and list detailed characteristics, attributes, and properties of the example.

4. Force combinations between these attributes and the problem statement(s) to provide exotic, bizarre ideas.

5. Turn each bizarre idea into realistic and workable ideas to solve the original problem. One way to do this: non-evaluatively list each characteristic, attribute, and property of the bizarre idea and force combinations between these and the problem. Be patient, and you will move toward new ways of viewing the problem and a high quality solution.

Like-Improve Analysis

Decide what you like about the problem area, so you won't change that, while you dissect out what's deficient and needs improvement. More logical than the problem-defining creativity triggers described above, and still very effective to shift paradigms and analyze problems.

Write your problem statement and list 'Things I Like' and

Things I Want Improved.

(Turn the improvements wanted into 'How to' statements.)

Reversal / De-Reversal

Turn your problem upside down. When you get right side up again, you will face a new direction after the paradigm shifts. Here's how:

Write your starting problem statement:
How to...

1. Reverse the key verb of the problem statement. For example: write quench instead of stimulate; decrease instead of increase; fail instead of succeed; etc.
2. Non-evaluatively list solutions to the reversed problem statement.
3. De-reverse by writing "How-to" in front of each solution.
4. Smooth out the wording of the new problem statement until it makes sense. Do this creatively.

Choose an appropriate new "How-to" problem statement to use during idea generation.

Restate the problem: How to …

Example of reversal-dereversal:
1. Reverse "How to stimulate creativity in your class" into "How to spoil creativity in your class."
2. One way to spoil creativity is: Have dominating students present.
3. De-reverse this statement to: "How to stay creative with dominating students present" or "How to get dominating students to stop dominating."
4. Choose the problem statement on which you'd like to focus.

Reverse Assumptions

Uncover the unwarranted assumptions you make about your problem and use them to discover new paradigms and novel 'How-to' problem statements.

1. Non-evaluatively list five to twenty assumptions you make about your problem. Include obvious assumptions you take for granted. Drop the unwarranted assumption that you can do this task easily.

2. Reverse the meaning of each assumption.

3. Non-evaluatively force combinations between each reversed assumption and your how-to problem statement. Produce bizarre and not-so-bizarre problem statements and ideas.

4. Select, combine, change, add to, and develop new How-to problem statements.

Fresh Eye

Take on a new identity. Think about how to solve your problem as someone or something else.

Write your starting problem statement:
How to...

How would you view your problem if you were a...

a) Dolphin, bat, eagle, jellyfish, pea pod, oak seed (choose one)
 How to...
b) Chemical engineer, mechanical engineer, Martian, artist (choose one)
    How to...
c) Biologist, chemist, secretary, banker, frog, geneticist (choose one)
    How to...
d) Architect, building contractor, carpenter, accountant, shark (choose one)
    How to...

e) Physicist, astronomer, musician, dancer, elephant, farmer (choose one)

How to...

f) Hydraulic engineer, clothes designer, trumpet player, cougar (choose one)

How to...

Restate your problem:

How to...

You should now have a multitude of new ways to see your problem.

Word Substitution

A systematic change of a word in a problem statement transforms perspectives profoundly. New paradigm shifts easily occur.   For example, you can transform "How to get rid of a dominating person"...into:

"How to get rid of a dominating person"
  "   " work with   "
  "   " change   "
  "   " succeed with   "
  "   " enjoy   "
  "   " do away with   "
  "   " handle   "
  "   " avoid   "
  "   " work around   "
  "   " succeed in spite of "
  "   " get along with   "
  "   " retrain   "
  "   " negotiate with," etc.

Note the different perspectives that occur with each verb substitution, which help you see new ways to approach this problem. Playing around with the word 'dominating' or 'person' may also provide a help-ful forced-withdrawal.

Why, Why, Why, Why, Why, And Why Again

Ask yourself WHY about the problem many times. This will force you to look at a problem in a different way. More logical than some other approaches, it still leads to unexpected new perspectives.

In addition, to asking WHY, follow this approach:

Write your starting problem statement:

How to...

Answer the following questions about the problem:

Why?

Who?

What?

Where?

When?

With whom?

Why, again?

Restate the problem: How to...

Needs, Obstacles, And Constraints

Force yourself to look at the problem in a different way.

List needs: What do you want?

How to achieve...

How to gain...

How to...

List obstacles: What is in the way?

How to overcome...

How to get around...

How to...

List constraints: What must you accept?
How to cope with...
How to substitute for...
How to...

When finished, write a new problem statement.
How to...

Weaknesses Of Quick-Fix Solutions

Get past pet solutions and old paradigms by examining their weaknesses.

Write your starting problem statement:
How to...

List three quick-fix solutions and some weaknesses of each one.

State the problem based on what you have written:
How to...

Use the problem-analyzing triggers described above in addition to the usual ways you use to analyze problems. Every problem-analyzing procedure helps reveal some aspect of the problem and shifts para-digms toward a quality solution.

RUNG #2. IDENTIFY THE CRITERIA TO SELECT YOUR HOW-TO PROBLEM STATE-MENT(S)

The following questions will help you identify the criteria to select problem statements on which you will focus:

Whose problem?

What does the problem involve?
    Students
    Faculty
    Classes
    Work
    Relationships
    Money
    Other

How big?
    Resources
    Students
    Time
    Fun

Other resources

Your gut feelings?
List the tangible and intangible values.

Other issues?

Check the kind of ideas you want...
( ) You want ideas that involve students.
( ) You want ideas that involve relationships.
( ) You want ideas for new plans.
( ) You want ideas for a new life.
( ) You want ideas that involve money.
( ) You want ideas for new paradigms, perspectives, and better ways to do things.
( ) Other kinds of ideas?

Non-evaluatively list the criteria you will use to choose the problem statement.

Write five to ten more How-to problem statements.

• CHAPTER 11 •
RUNG #3.
CHOOSE THE HOW-TO
PROBLEM STATEMENTS
THAT YOU WANT TO SOLVE

RUNG #3. CHOOSE THE HOW-TO PROBLEM STATEMENTS THAT YOU WANT TO SOLVE

Focus on more than one How-to problem statement to make sure you do not miss anything important. Write three problem statements.

How to...

How to...

How to...

Choose the leading problem statement.

How to...

• CHAPTER 12 •
RUNG #4:
GENERATE NEW IDEAS
WHILE SOLVING PROBLEMS
ALONE

(THE 2ND KEY CREATIVE RUNG
ON THE LADDER)

"Brainstorming doesn't accomplish enough any more ...
too old fashioned."

RUNG #4: GENERATE NEW IDEAS *ALONE*

FIRST: SEEK HOW-TO PROBLEM STATEMENTS

Have you got your chosen How-to problem statements lined up? If not, start by generating numerous "How to" problem statements (not less than 10, although 25 is better) using the creativity triggers described in Chapter 9.

If you wish, record these on regular sheet of paper. However, I prefer to move around writing on large flip chart paper on an easel or the wall. This movement seems to help my creative thinking.

Or you may record ideas on index cards, one idea per card to facilitate sorting.

Check the five to ten How-to problem statements that you find most interesting and impacting. From these, choose three quite different problem statements to tackle.

A PRODUCTIVE SEQUENCE OF IDEA-GENERATING TRIGGERS WHILE WORK-ING _ALONE_

Now start using this proven sequence of the idea-generating triggers to create ideas (rung 4) when solving problems **alone**.

The ideas you generate using this sequence will astonish you with their unexpectedness, freshness, and usefulness. Each creativity trigger in the sequence builds on the previous one and reaches into higher levels of creative thinking. Expect amazement and delight at the outcome, an explosion of unique ideas.

Brainstorming / Non-Evaluative Listing

Brainstorming was popularized over 80 years ago, and we have invented hundreds of newer and more effective triggers to enhance idea-generation since then. Still, use brainstorming to help you flush obvious pet ideas from old paradigms and clear your mind for higher levels of creative thinking using more advanced creativity triggers.

During brainstorming, write all ideas quickly on a note pad. Do not evaluate. Do not hesitate. Write ideas twice. Do not worry about spelling, grammar, or repetition. Write them all. Brainstorming generally produces many low-level ideas.

A number of useful variations exist. Brainstorm for three minutes; rest for three minutes; brainstorm for another three minutes, etc.

Effective outcomes during brainstorming depend on remaining non-evaluative. Evaluation comes from old information. When we evaluate, we immerse ourselves in old thoughts and paradigms.

To escape from old perspectives, stay non-evaluative. I stress this point by calling the process 'Non-Evaluative Listing' and suggest the following guidelines:

- List all ideas.
- Do not think about items.
- Do not evaluate.

- Ignore repetition. Write the idea down again.
- Write bizarre ideas.
- Defer judgment and postpone evaluations until later.
- Keep the process moving.
- Do not hesitate

Start generating ideas using non-evaluative listing (brainstorming). It records your pet ideas, and you will stop worrying that you will forget these ideas. Also, it flushes out and clears the mind of obvious solutions and makes room so advanced creativity triggers work even better. However, if you want to produce a high quality solution, non-evaluative thinking (or brainstorming) won't get you there. Consider it, at best, a nice warm-up procedure.

The opposite of non-evaluative listing encompasses the 'gauntlet.' when you internally filter your own idea.

Even if you use the gauntlet only 10% of the time, it results in 100% gauntlet. In other words, even if you only evaluate one idea out of ten, you will suppress many of your ideas.

A HABIT THAT SPOILS CREATIVITY: The **gauntlet**. You need total non-evaluative thinking when listing ideas. You can achieve this with a little practice.

Non-evaluatively list ideas for one of the How-to problem statements you chose. After a few minutes, include some silly, bizarre ideas. When you run out of ideas for one problem statement, start the non-evaluative listing process on another. Work on at least three quite different How-to problem statements.

Improve Bizarre Trigger-Ideas

Non-evaluatively list at least fifteen bizarre and absurd ideas to solve a problem statement. Stay really bizarre. No one watches you when you work alone.

Then combine the most bizarre ideas and use the outcome as a trigger to spark a better idea. In other words, turn the bears and the pots of honey into helicopters (Chapter 5) or the weak seam of the pea pod into the weak seam to open a can (Chapter 9). Use the bizarre ideas ingeniously to provoke useful ideas.

Finally, fold blank flip chart papers into different shapes and use them unfolded as the bizarre trigger-ideas to spark better ideas. Even the blank unfolded paper sparks an active imagination at this stage, and all sorts of interesting ideas emerge. Also use driftwood or strangely shaped rocks to spark ideas.

Weird To The Workable Idea

Fold a sheet of paper into four equal quadrants. Then think weirdly and create a very weird idea. Write it in the first quadrant. Make the idea as exotic and bizarre as possible.

Use the weird idea to trigger a better idea and write it in the second quadrant.

Use the better idea to trigger a practical idea and write it in the third quadrant.

Finally, use the practical idea to trigger a workable idea and write it in the fourth quadrant. Turn this idea into a sensible, practical solution.

Repeat as needed. The more bizarre and weird the first idea, the more likely you will produce an unexpected and unusual workable idea at the end, a paradigm shift.

Idea Gallery

Write four to six How-to problem statements that interest you at the top of sheets of flip chart paper, one statement per sheet. Attach the papers to the wall creating an idea gallery.

Walk around the room and write ideas directly on the papers. The ideas that accumulate on the papers will trigger other ideas as you wander around. Such movement often helps creative thinking. Ask others to contribute ideas. Expect unexpected ideas.

Variation: Hang sheet of flip chart paper in the hall outside your room. Write one How-to problem statement on the top. Ask each passersby to write ideas on the flip chart paper.

Free Word Association Imagery

Free word association imagery produces few ideas that are most unusual. Be patient. This creativity trigger takes time and practice.

Choose a vibrant problem statement. Intuitively select a dynamic word from that statement. Then forget the problem. Write a one-word free association to the chosen word. Then write a one-word free association to the new word. Continue writing a one-word free association to each new word generated for at least six successive words.

Intuitively select one of the words. Close your eyes, and spend a few minutes forming images around the chosen word (you may even meditate). After a few minutes, list the images on paper. Repeat this process with another word.

Then force exotic and bizarre combinations between the images and your chosen problem statement. Make them impractical, absurd, outrageous, and utterly weird.

Finally, use these bizarre image combinations to trigger practical ideas. Non-evaluatively list these ideas on flip chart paper and develop them into proposals that spark sensible, workable solutions for the original problem statement. Improve the ideas. Repeat the process. Expect unique ideas that sparkle.

ANOTHER FORCED COMBINATION: Take an imaginary trip to Africa or Venus and bring back something absurd to combine with the problem at hand. Also use imaginary objects from Asia or Mars as creativity triggers to spark unexpected ideas.

Idea Card

Finally, sit quietly for about 30-40 minutes and write one idea per card on 5" x 8" index cards using a dark marker. Stay non-evaluative as you write your ideas. Use the principles found in non-evaluative listing and automatic writing. Occasionally write absurd, bizarre, exotic ideas and use these to spark other ideas. Expect many unexpected ideas to emerge on these cards.

Place the cards on tables, on the floor, or pin them to a wall so you can see them all. Sort them. Idea board described in Chapter 13 jazzes up idea sorting.

A SUCCESS STORY: Idea card combined with automatic writing is superbly suited to enhance idea generation. My friend, Vicki Bradley, went quietly berserk after she learned this procedure, non-evaluatively writing every idea she had on index cards, pieces of paper, napkins, etc. A very creative artist, musician, and craftsperson, she claims idea card increased her creative output manyfold. I believe her.

ADDITIONAL CREATIVITY TRIGGERS, WHEN NEEDED

The sequence described above will yield ideas galore, more than enough to solve most problems. If not, repeat the sequence, or if you wish, move on to the following idea-generating triggers.

Combining Logical And Bizarre Ideas

Combine idea gallery with idea card to create a variation of combining-ideas groups described below. Allot at least 45-60 minutes for this creativity trigger.

In the first 15 minutes, create bizarre and silly ideas only and non-evaluatively list these on flip chart paper. In the next 15 minutes, generate only logical solutions that make sense and non-evaluatively list these on 3" x 5" index cards, one idea per card.

Finally, combine and force combinations between the ideas of the two lists and develop new, unexpected ideas. Expect it to work. It will.

Dream Interruption Brainwriting

Outline the problem using no more than five sentences. Put a pencil and a pad of paper next to your bed. At bed time, review the outline. Tell yourself that you will obtain solutions to the problem, that you know you have the solution somewhere in your mind, and that you will wake yourself up when everything fits together.

Very likely, you will probably wake up with fertile, unexpected thoughts. Jot them down at once or you will forget them. This procedure works best when you anticipate great outcomes.

This approach works well when you want something rich. I could easily use a quick fix, but by doing it this way, I get a lot of depth, some unconventional ideas, and many trigger-ideas. I have to really want to do it. I have to enter into this procedure with anticipation and wonderment of impending greatness that will somehow be realized before morning."

Brainwriting Clusters

Use this trigger spontaneously in a free-writing way.

Sit with your group. The recorder writes a nucleus-word representing your problem in the center of a piece of paper or on a flip chart so all can see. Draw a circle around it.

Write rapidly whatever comes to mind in a cluster of words or short phrases around the core nucleus-word. Draw a circle around each word or thought as you write it and link it to the previous circle. This forms a series of words inside linked circles to form a flow chart of ideas.

Do not think about what you write. Do free intuitive writing. Don't seek connectedness. You want randomness in the early stages. Go off on wild tangents. Shift paradigms. Look for different mind ruts. Seek the bizarre. Stay non-evaluative.

Cluster phrases and words in linked circles around interesting thoughts. Write clusters of words and phrases in linked circles as long as ideas flow freely. When you run out of ideas, stop a while before you add new words or thoughts.

Study the cluster of words and phrases in the linked circles you created. Non-evaluatively list ideas you might want to try. Draw lines between word clusters to form new, synergetic approaches to the problem. Show the clusters of words to someone else to trigger new ideas.

Set a quota for a minimum number of ideas. Settling for less than five new ideas accepts the obvious, the quick fix.

To force combinations between unrelated concepts, use two or more word-nuclei at opposite corners of the same page. This will force a combination or create a usable metaphor between these concepts as you fill the page.

Brainwriting Circles

A useful variation of clustering.

The recorder writes a word or phrase that captures the spirit of the problem in a small circle in the center of a blank sheet of paper on a writing pad or on an easel. Write an entire "How-to" problem statement if you wish.

Write words close to the circle that you associate with the concept within the circle. Use the non-evaluative listing and automatic writing principles in a process of progressive free association.

When no more room exists next to the circle, move outward a bit and form a new circle. Continue filling the page with concentric circles of words triggered by free association with the original word or phrase, or with any of the words and phrases that you write on the paper.

Stay creative throughout. Use linear and nonlinear creative thinking. Do not evaluate. Go off on tangents. The words you write do not have to connect or make sense.

After you fill the paper, make connections and remote connections by circling and drawing lines between words or phrases that define patterns of new paradigms and ideas that seem useful in themselves or as triggers to new ideas. Use different colored pencils or pens. Make creative connections.

Stay patient. Allow this process to work. It may seem fragile, about to shatter into a useless jumble. Carefully nurture it by not forcing the words and phrases to make sense too soon. Stay with it. This procedure can help your creative thinking in marvelous ways.

Insert Other Creativity Triggers
Into This Sequence

Use the sequence of idea-generating triggers described above. Allot enough time so you can do justice to creative thinking. Seize opportunities working alone.

What can you do if **no** ideas occur to you, and your mind is a blank? Use automatic writing described in Chapter 4 to unblock your block and regain your creativeness. Or insert some of the idea triggers that follow.

USE FORCED COMBINATIONS AND
TRIGGER-IDEAS

Force combinations between your idea and other objects to create additional new ideas. Combine remote connections and watch your creative thinking take off.

Forced-combinations help new ideas appear by mixing the characteristics and properties of two or more objects or thoughts to spark remote connections. The clock radio illustrates a familiar outcome of forced-combination.

Here's an example of a forced-combination between unrelated stimuli. Open a book. Point randomly to any word. List all the properties and characteristics of this word. Combine these properties and your problem to spark new ideas to solve it. Amazingly this quick-fix approach works well.

When you combine very **unrelated** items and thoughts, you produce very original ideas. However, these new ideas often prove difficult to turn into practical, workable solutions. **Related** stimuli and trigger-ideas usually produce less novel ideas more easily used.

Make additional forced-combinations this way:

1, Non-evaluatively list characteristics, connections, reminders, and properties of the trigger-idea.

2. Write your problem statement. How to...

3. Non-evaluatively list the ideas from the forced combination between your problem and the trigger-idea.

Analogies As Trigger-Ideas

Want exceptional outcomes?

1. Choose a culture, civilization, profession, country, group, organization, animal, or plant.

2. Non-evaluatively list the characteristics of the culture, civilization, profession, group, country, organization, animal, or plant.

3. Write your problem statement. How to...

4. Non-evaluatively list the ideas from the forced combinations between the characteristics and your problem statement.

Metaphors As Trigger-Ideas

Metaphors open your mind. Try this.

1. Study an object, situation, or picture.

2. Non-evaluatively list specific characteristics or properties, such as color, shape, texture, odor, feel, sound, taste, composition, etc.

3. Choose one property or characteristic. Non-evaluatively list what that property or characteristic reminds you of. For example, a 'WHITE PAGE IN A BOOK' is... snow; smooth silk; a flat table top; speckled ash on snow; a lined, plowed field; etc.

4. Non-evaluatively list the characteristics, nuances, impressions, and properties of your metaphor.

5. Force-combinations between the items in '4' above with your problem statement.

6. Select, combine, change, add to, and develop an idea to help generate a quality solution.

7. Improve your idea by non-evaluatively listing, in turn, what you like and can use in your idea; deficiencies that need improving; and ways you can overcome the deficiencies.

8. Use the process again using a new metaphor. Expect good results and you will get them.

Metaphors, Poetry, And Creative Thinking

Use metaphors to write poems about the problem area. For example, suppose you want to improve a BLACK MAGIC MARKER. Examine its characteristics.
- IT HAS BLACK INK, like...a squid, a pen, swamp water.
- IT IS BLACK, like...midnight, a dark mood, black paint.
- IT HAS A SLEEK SHAPE, like...a bullet, rocket, racing car.
- IT HAS A COVER CAP, like...a cap on a tooth paste tube.
- IT STANDS UPRIGHT, like...a tree, space shuttle, chimney, an open playpen.
- IT LIES DOWN, like...an airplane landing, chopsticks on a table.
- IT IS SHINY, like...patent leather, an apple, a mirror.
  Combine these analogies & metaphors into a poem...

"Ode To A Black Magic Marker In A Creative Thinking Workshop"

"IN A DARK MOOD,
THE MIDNIGHT BULLET ROCKETS THROUGH THE PLAYPEN,
EXPLODING, LIKE AN INK-FILLED SQUID,
INTO TRIGGERS BIZARRE."

In this poem, "playpen" is a metaphor for the workshop, while the bullet (the magic marker) explodes into triggers (of ideas), the reverse of firing a gun where the trigger provokes the explosion of the bullet.

Write poems in a similar way about your problem statement. This procedure opens up new perspectives and stimulates the kind of creative thinking that leads to quality solutions.

Pictures As Trigger-Ideas

Choose a picture to trigger new ideas. Non-evaluatively list all visual elements in the picture. Force combinations between specific visual elements and specific elements of the problem. Make remote connections that help devise quality solutions to solve your problem. Use visual triggers from any source and watch your creative thinking soar.

Random Words As Trigger-Ideas

Combine non-relevant ideas with your How-to problem statement to spark creative remote connections. Put your finger at random on any word below and force combinations between it and your problem statement to generate new paradigms, new problem statements, and new ideas.

• bears, television, cup and saucer, pea pods, mountains, baseball, bamboo, car, Idaho, clock, telephone, tennis ball, sofa, waterfalls, skiing, dancing, football, Ohio, car, book, house, radio, museum, wine, pencil, watermelon, town, countryside, pen, lamp, cooking, electricity, outer space, pole vault, jokes, sculpture, fishing, candle, rock, Kansas, cows, laugh, joy, fun, toys, dreams, sewing, automobile, religion, laser beam, dice, magic, winter, NYC, meditation, children, rock-and-roll, astronomy, love, movies, watch, money, friend, school, mountain, laughter, flying, ocean, key, street, store, knife, universe, home, boxing, horses, painting, love, swing.

Book Pages As Trigger-Ideas

Use a random word from a book as an idea trigger.

Write down a page number and another number chosen at random. Choose a book. Turn to the page you listed and count words up to the number you listed. Force combinations between that word and your problem statement. Generate new problem statements and new ideas. Simple, flexible, and effective.

Quotations As Trigger-Ideas

Force combinations using your favorite quotations.

1. Non-evaluatively list 10-20 famous quotations.

2. Choose a quotation that seems to evoke a strong response.

3. Write your quotation....

4. Non-evaluatively list the quotation's characteristics, properties, impressions, nuances, values, etc.

5. Write your 'How-to problem statement. How to...

6. Force combinations between the characteristics of your quotation and your problem statement. Non-evaluatively list the ideas that come to mind.

7. Select, combine, change, add to, slice, and develop the ideas to solve your problem.

8. Improve your idea. List its characteristics and properties.

   (a) Non-evaluatively list what you like and can use in your idea.

   (b) Non-evaluatively list deficiencies that need improving in your idea. Convert these into How-to problem statements.

   (c) Non-evaluatively list ways to improve your idea by solving the problem statements in '8(b)' above.

9. Repeat the entire process. Allow good results to happen.

Idea Grid

Use idea grid, a systematic search for new perspectives and paradigms, to make sure you did not overlook anything.

Example: "How to improve creative thinking in your college?"

1. Draw a grid.

2. Fill in the top and the first side row with categories relating to the main problem.

3. Force combinations between categories to generate new ideas in each box.

Please fill out the 'idea grid' on the next page.

Please write at least one idea in each category below. If you find some categories not relevant, please change them. Think of other problems that you can solve using Idea Grid.

	How to Increase the Quality of New Ideas	How to Increase the Quantity of New Ideas	How to Help Improve New Ideas	How to Increase the Development of New Ideas	How to Improve the Implementation of New Ideas	How to Improve Screening and Selection of New Ideas
In Meetings						
In Yourself						
In Your Class						
In Your Peers						
In Your School						
In the Faculty						
In Your Department						
In the Administration						

CREATIVITY TRIGGERS INVOLVING FUTURE FANTASY

Future fantasy produces the most unexpected, creative, highest quality solutions to complex problems. This approach combines expectations of the future with current reality. Use this approach only with an experienced creative thinking group.

What-If / Future Fantasy Year

A very advanced creativity trigger that requires practice and lots of time. This creativity trigger was originally designed for groups working on this together. Therefore, it may overwhelm you if you go it alone. Be patient and methodical. Pretend you play a game of solitaire.

If you work on this by yourself, plan to spend time on it each day for many days, even a week. Nonetheless, it can yield the most unusual, unexpected, and useful solutions, Expect startling results.

Write your problem statement. How to...

Fantasize the future when someone solved your problem.
List each of the following items on separate pages without thinking about the possible solution.

1. Non-evaluatively list those people inside and outside your school who **gained** by the success.

2. Non-evaluatively list those people who **lost** now that someone solved the problem.

3. Non-evaluatively list the 'Fantasy Resource People' you brought in to help create and implement the solution. These include...

• Experts from the past and present.

• Experts from other colleges and corporations.

• Experts or animals from Sea World, Kennedy Space Center, or Epcot Center.

• Experts or heroes, historical or mythological, to help.

• Fantasy helpers: writers, scientists, artists, inventors, thinkers, business students, professors, consultants, CEOs, etc.

4. For each person or animal listed in #3 above, non-evaluatively list specifically what each uniquely does in the future to help create and implement the successful solution. Start each item with the name of the person or animal.

5. Use each activity listed in #4 above as a trigger-idea to spark new ideas to solve your problem as it exists today. Force combinations between these trigger-ideas and your problem statement.

6. Improve each idea using idea-improvement triggers.

Future Fantasy Year produces a cascade of trigger-ideas, thus:

Other people and animals =>
    Unique activities =>
        Unexpected new & useful ideas

Allow four to ten (many, many) hours for this very advanced procedure. Don't rush it because it seems non-logical. Logic will play a role, never fear. This creativity trigger: so powerful, an explosion of uniqueness.

IF YOU WISH, JUMP TO CHAPTER 17 TO READ ABOUT IDEA-GENERATING TRIGGERS FOR STUDENTS WHO SOLVE PROBLEMS CREATIVELY IN _GROUPS_

• CHAPTER 13 •
RUNG #5.
COMBINE IDEAS INNOVATIVELY INTO
CREATIVE TRIGGER-PROPOSALS

(THE 3RD KEY CREATIVE RUNG
ON THE LADDER)

RUNG #5. COMBINE IDEAS INNOVATIVELY INTO
CREATIVE TRIGGER-PROPOSALS

It's time to select the best idea(s). Creativity stops when you evaluate, but wait! Behold a creativity trigger that allows you to re-main creative and still sort and evaluate ideas. This chapter deals with Rung #5 of the eight-rung problem-solving sequence described in Chapter 9.

FORCED WITHDRAWAL

Evaluation uses old information to judge new ideas, so you quickly discard ideas that seem unworkable. (the quick automatic No). This reduces your chances for a high quality solution when selecting ideas. Yet, you can convert this normally evaluative (non-creative) rung into one that creates new possibilities instead of diminishing them.

One antidote to this difficulty: forced withdrawal. Trick your mind. Pretend you solve the problem with a fresh look as someone or something else.

Combine ideas into a trigger-proposal to solve your problem in a new school, not your current one, or in a new organization or another country.

Trigger-proposals keep you from committing to an idea too soon, avoiding the quick fix. This unique process allows you to review and combine ideas you might prematurely reject and thus miss out on a high-quality solution.

This approach keeps you from applying criteria too soon, and allows you to stay creative as you select and combine ideas. Also, it keeps you from using unstated, phantom criteria. Finally, it prevents you from stifling your own ideas with thoughts such as "they tried that before" or "I'll never get them to agree," a typical student tactic.

For example, suppose you want to develop a quality solution on: "How to stimulate creative thinking in yourself." Let's pretend you have generated 100 ideas for this How-to problem statement. You are now at Rung #5 of the problem-solving ladder.

Use these ideas to prepare an innovative one-page trigger-proposal on how to stimulate creative thinking in another person (forced withdrawal).

1. Pretend you are someone else (write his or her name here).

2. Look over the ideas generated during the idea-generating sessions of Rung #4. Combine, modify, add to, subtract from, connect, and change them.

3. List ideas you like on 3" x 5" index cards, one idea per card. Then non-evaluatively list new ideas about what you might include in a trigger-proposal on 3" x 5" index cards, one idea per card. Let the ideas flow. Let your imagination soar. Stay very creative.

4. Sort the cards. Place the ideas in the sequence you want.

5. Summarize them on one page to generate your trigger-proposal. Think very creatively.

• CHAPTER 14 •
RUNG #6.
IDENTIFY CRITERIA FOR YOUR
QUALITY SOLUTION

RUNG #6: IDENTIFY THE CRITERIA
TO CHOOSE A HIGH QUALITY SOLUTION

Before you can develop a quality solution, you must identify the criteria you will use to choose it. Do this with great care and thoughtful reflection. After the effort you put into all those creativity triggers, produce a high quality solution. Don't let unstated, phantom criteria spoil your quality outcome. Use the following list to help identify the important criteria:

Ease of implementation

Consequences of doing nothing

Tangible costs:
    materials
    equipment
    space
    people

Intangible costs:
    opinions
    attitudes
    feelings
    Aesthetics

Difficulties of implementation

Compatible with your group and your college

Marketability to others

Effect on your overall goals

Individuals and groups affected

Moral and legal implications

New problems caused

Consequences of success and failure

Timeliness

Benefits to you, your group, and your school

Satisfy others who have to agree

Your gut feelings

Other issues...

Write the criteria you will use to select ideas and develop into proposals and solutions.

• CHAPTER 15 •
RUNG #7.
CONVERT YOUR TRIGGER-PROPOSAL INTO A
QUALITY SOLUTION

Develop a fresh, high-quality solution by applying your trigger-proposal to solve your real problem.

Idea Board

I learned this procedure from William Drath at the Center For Creative Leadership. Write your ideas on 5" x 8" index cards with a magic marker, and arrange them on a large bulletin board according to themes and categories, one idea per card, and one theme or category per column.

Make sure you can see the writing from a distance. Attach the cards with pins, or for greater ease when arranging the cards, use a magnetic board with magnetized buttons.

Use the idea board to help sort and categorize the many ideas generated during idea card described in Chapter 12.

Also use idea board to display a specific planning process so you can easily see the steps in a plan, and can add new steps in sequence.

Organize the cards in vertical columns on the idea board. Create headings for each column that include all the cards under it.

Use different colored cards for different purposes. For example, use yellow cards for general headings and write the ideas on orange cards. Use blue cards to head the column of ideas you have put aside, but not yet rejected, while green cards can head the column of ideas that you think clear winners.

Generate new ideas and new headings as needed. Develop a creative trigger-proposal and a sensible solution that fits your criteria.

STRUCTURE IS IMPORTANT WHEN GOING AFTER QUALITY SOLUTIONS

By now you might wonder about my emphasis on structure throughout this book. Isn't creative thinking usually a helter-skelter free-for-all? In reality, it may seem that way, but as my friend, Bob Phillips, pointed out, creative thinking flourishes best for many students within specific structures using special discipline. The intense focus and tuning-out of extraneous stimuli necessary for creative thinking require structure and enforced discipline, not to box the creative person in, but to keep out unwanted distraction and interfering stimuli.

The special conditions vary with the person (see 'personal creativity environments' in Chapter 1). Deliberately set up the structure, stick to it, and relentlessly protect it from breaking down by keeping distractions and interruptions from interfering with the creative process. Assert and say NO to spoilers of creative thinking around you. Don't let the stiflers of creative thinking overwhelm you and prevent you from producing a quality solution.

• CHAPTER 16 •
RUNG #8.
READY, SET, ACTION PLANS

RUNG #8. READY, SET, ACTION PLANS

Achieving quality solutions involves a probabilities game. Increase the probabilities that you will:
- analyze the problem and shift paradigms innovatively,
- generate useful ideas super-abundantly,
- combine ideas into creative trigger-proposals,
- identify criteria appropriately,
- convert trigger-proposals into outstanding quality solutions,
- make effective action plans.

The payoff in excellence makes this effort worthwhile. You accomplish so much more after you make specific action plans containing detailed action plans.

Who Does What, Where, When, How, And Why?

Please fill out the Action Plan Form on the following page:

Action Plan Regarding...

	Action Plan 1.	Action Plan 2.	Action Plan 3.
	i	i	i
What is to be done?			
Who does it?			
When?			
Where?			
Why?			
What else?			

NOW READ ABOUT IDEA-GENERATING TRIGGERS FOR STUDENTS WHO SOLVE PROBLEMS CREATIVELY IN _GROUPS_ IN CHAPTER 17, NEXT.

• PART 4 •
FOR STUDENTS WHO SOLVE PROBLEMS CREATIVELY IN _GROUPS_

Creativity triggers sharpen your competitive edge.

• CHAPTER 17 •
RUNG #4 again:
GENERATE IDEAS TO SOLVE PROBLEMS CREATIVELY IN _GROUPS_

(THE 2ND KEY CREATIVE RUNG IN THE LADDER, again)

"Brainstorming doesn't accomplish enough any more ... too old-fashioned."

RUNG #4: IDEA-GENERATING TRIGGERS FOR STUDENTS WHO SOLVE PROBLEMS CREATIVELY IN _GROUPS_

The creativity triggers described in Part 3 of this book for students who solve problems **alone** also apply to students who solve problems in **groups**.

However, idea generation (Rung 4) in groups requires special discussion. That's what this chapter is about.

Working in groups has many benefits. There is a diversity of knowledge, expertise, interest, background, and skills to draw on that helps enormously. The extent to which a group produces new ideas depends on the creative climate and how the group encourages new ideas.

Still, groups do not generate ideas. Individuals do, so good relationships within the group must prevail. This part of the book also touches on how to maintain good interactions and a creative climate.

For a more detailed description on how to insure effective interactions and a creative climate in groups, see Chapter 27 in my book: "TEAM CREATIVITY AT WORK I & II: Creative Problem Solving At Its Best,"

BRAINSTORMING TRIGGERS

Brainstorming in groups was popularized over 80 years ago, and we have invented hundreds of newer and more effective triggers to enhance idea generation since then. Still, brainstorming helps you flush obvious pet ideas from old paradigms and clear your mind for higher levels of creative thinking using more advanced triggers.

During brainstorming, a recorder writes all ideas on a note pad or flip chart paper for all to see, while everyone withholds evaluation. It generally produces many ideas.

A number of useful variations exist. For example: brainstorm for three minutes; be quiet for three minutes; brainstorm for another three minutes, etc.

Or, after a while, go around the group in order, each person taking turns to express one idea. This allows timid people the space to contribute.

Non-Evaluative Listing

Effective outcomes during brainstorming depend on everyone remaining non-evaluative. Evaluation uses old information. When we evaluate, we immerse ourselves in old paradigms.

To escape from old perspectives, stay non-evaluative. I stress this point by calling the process 'Non-Evaluative Listing' and suggest the following guidelines:

- List all ideas.
- Do not think about items.
- Do not evaluate.
- Ignore repetition. Write the idea down again.
- Write bizarre ideas.
- Defer judgment and postpone evaluations until later.
- Keep the process moving.
- Do not hesitate.

First, select the How-to problem statements on which the group will focus. Then start the idea-generating session with non-evaluative listing (brainstorming) because it records everyone's pet ideas and participants stop worrying they will lose these ideas. Also, non-evaluative listing flushes out and clears the mind of obvious solutions and makes room so advanced creative thinking triggers work even better.

However, if you want to produce a high quality solution, non-evaluative thinking (or brainstorming) won't get you there. Consider it, at best, a nice warm-up.

Recorder's Roles

Additional important recorder's roles include:
- Reminds the group to stick to non-evaluative listing.
- Keeps loud members from dominating the group.
- Encourages quiet members.
- Does not discuss ideas.
- Writes down bizarre ideas.
- Plays subdued leadership roles.
- Acts as a 'servant' to the group.

The opposite of non-evaluative listing encompasses the 'gauntlet,' when you internally filter your own idea.

Even if you use the gauntlet only 10% of the time, it results in 100% gauntlet. In other words, even if you only evaluate one idea out of ten, you will suppress many ideas.

A HABIT THAT SPOILS CREATIVITY: The **gauntlet**. You need total non-evaluation when listing ideas. You can achieve this with a little practice.

Buzz Groups

Use this antidote to the quick fix during meetings. Especially useful when you want many ideas in a meeting without a long discussion.

One person presents a problem. Teams of four to six people turn in their seats to form small 'buzz groups' where they sit. Each 'buzz' group quickly chooses a recorder, who non-evaluatively lists ideas on a writing pad for five minutes. The recorder quickly reads them aloud and gives the list to the presenter of the problem for future use. If the problem-presenter merely says, "Thank you" and does not get into a discussion, the total time takes less than fifteen minutes.

One variation: first ask the buzz groups to non-evaluatively list How-to problem statements. Then one or more of these are chosen by the presenter of the problem for the buzz group to use during idea generation. See Chapter 18 for an excellent use of buzz groups.

A TRUE STORY: In one of my workshops, a manager said he wanted to restructure work groups to eliminate the supervisors and have teams of workers led by temporary team leaders. Most people favored it except the local union, who insisted everyone get the same pay raise as the team leaders.

I formed three buzz groups with the 18 people present, and while they listed ideas, the plant manager and I privately agreed that, at most, he might get some trigger-ideas to spark ideas at some later time.

To our delight, the participants generated over 40 ideas, three of which when combined, yielded a solution that he thought would satisfy

---

the union. Because of its incentive orientation, he expected to increase productivity while reducing supervisor costs. The plant manager beamed. "Trust the process," we concluded

BRAINWRITING TRIGGERS

By 1970, research had shown that students who sit privately writing their own ideas generated more ideas as a group than a comparable team using brainstorming.

Idea Gallery Brainwriting

Write six to ten How-to problem statements at the top of flip chart papers, one problem statement per sheet. Attach the flip chart papers to the wall for idea gallery.

Walk around and write ideas and solutions directly on the sheets of paper. The ideas that accumulate on the paper frequently trigger ideas as you wander around.

Try this variation. Hang a paper with a How-to problem statement written at the top outside your door and invite others to write their ideas. Some useful ideas will appear.

Idea Card Brainwriting

Sit quietly in your group for about 30-40 minutes, and write one idea per card on 5" x 8" colored index cards with a dark marker so you can read it easily. Do not evaluate your ideas. Use the non-evaluative listing and automatic writing principles. Occasionally write an absurd, bizarre exotic idea to trigger other ideas.

Relax now and then. Look your cards and allow a written idea to spark new ideas. Record the first idea that comes to mind when looking at each card.

An interesting variation: ask everyone to write an absurd, bizarre exotic idea on an index card. Pass the idea card to the student on your right. Write down the first idea that comes to your mind as you read the idea on the card you received. Use that idea as a trigger-idea to spark a better idea.

Another variation: Idea card can help produce an outline for a class report or talk. Non-evaluatively list the ideas you would like to include on 3" x 5" index cards, one idea per card. Sort your cards in the order you want them to appear in your report or talk. Now prepare your report or talk.

Improve Bizarre Trigger-Ideas Game

The purpose of this game: To stimulate each person to stretch his or her imagination and express bizarre trigger-ideas beyond previous levels. In addition, to give a creative thinking team the experience of helping to develop an idea no matter how bizarre so it becomes useful. The game has simple rules.

Each team has four minutes to generate the most bizarre, outrageous, and absurd idea to solve the problem. They pass this idea to another team.

That other team has four minutes to use this idea as a trigger to spark a better idea. In other words, turn the bears and the pots of honey into helicopters (Chapter 5), or turn the weak seam of the pea pod into the weak seam of a can (Chapter 9). If the team does so, it gets one point. If it does not, the other team gets one point. Expect many unexpected ideas.

Weird To Workable Idea

The recorder of each creative thinking team divides a large flip chart paper into four equal quadrants with a dark marker.

Each creative thinking team records a very "weird" idea to solve their problem statement in the first quadrant. They make the idea as exotic, absurd, and bizarre as possible. They pass the flip chart paper to another team.

This team uses the weird idea to trigger a "better" idea and write it in the second quadrant of the flip chart paper. They pass the flip chart paper to another team.

This team uses the better idea to trigger a "practical" idea and writes it in the third quadrant of the flip chart paper. They pass the flip chart paper to another team.

This team uses the practical idea to trigger a "workable" idea, writes it in the fourth quadrant of the flip chart paper, and turns the idea into a sensible, practical solution.

In general, the more bizarre and weird the first idea, the more likely the final workable idea captures the unexpected, original, and creative.

A FORCED-COMBINATION: Take an imaginary trip to Africa or Venus and bring back something absurd to forcibly combine with the R&D problem. Also, try Asia or Mars as a source of trigger-ideas.

Force combinations between your idea and other objects to produce additional new ideas. Combine remote connections and watch your creative thinking take off.

Free Word Association Imagery

This creativity trigger generates relatively few ideas, but the uniqueness of those ideas makes this trigger a gem. Expect many paradigm shifts. Use five to six students in a group plus a recorder

1. The recorder intuitively selects a dynamic word from the chosen problem statement.

2. The students do not focus on the problem. Instead, one person says a one-word free association to the chosen word. Each team member, in turn, says a one-word free association to the word generated by the preceding person. The recorder lists all the words.

3. The recorder intuitively picks one of the words. Students close their eyes and spend a few minutes imaging around the chosen word.

Students describe their images, which the recorder non-evaluatively lists on flip chart paper.

4. Students force exotic and bizarre combinations between the images and the problem statement.

5. Students use the bizarre combinations to spark practical ideas. The recorder non-evaluatively lists these on flip chart paper. Students develop a proposal and a potential sensible, workable solution for the original problem.

Repeat the process many times. Expect good results.

Combining-Ideas Teams

An excellent idea-generating procedure for an advanced creative thinking group.

1. Form three types of groups consisting of five to six students.

2. Designate one type as the 'logical group,' one type as the 'creative thinking group,' and the third type as the 'combining-ideas' group.

3. The 'combining-ideas' group remains idle while the 'logical' and the 'creative thinking' groups generate ideas to solve a given How-to problem statement using non-evaluating listing and idea card, about 20-30 minutes for each procedure.

4. Tell the 'creative thinking' group to focus on bizarre and wild ideas.

5. Tell the 'logical' group to concentrate only on logical ideas that make sense.

6. Tell the 'combining-ideas' group to force combinations between the ideas of the 'creative' and 'logical' teams, and develop new creative workable solutions.

A variation of this approach: form only two types of groups, the 'creative' and 'logical' groups, and ask them to force combinations between each other's ideas in mixed 'buzz groups.'

Idea grid

Use idea grid, a systematic search for new perspectives and para-digms, to make sure you did not overlook anything.

Example: "How to improve creative thinking in your college?"

1. Draw a grid.

2. Fill in the top and the first side row with categories relating to the main problem.

3. Force combinations between categories to generate new ideas in each box.

Please fill out the 'Idea Grid' on the next page.

Please write at least one idea in each category below. If you find some categories not relevant, please change them. Think of other problems that you can solve using Idea Grid.

	How to Increase The Quality of New Ideas	How to Increase The Quantity of New Ideas	How to Help Improve New Ideas	How to Increase The Development of New Ideas	How to Improve The Implementation of New Ideas	How to Improve Screening and Selection of New Ideas
In Meetings						
In Yourself						
In Your Class						
In Your Peers						
In Your School						
In the Faculty						
In Your Department						
In the Administration						

CREATIVITY TRIGGERS INVOLVING FUTURE FANTASY

Future fantasy produces the most unexpected, creative, highest quality solutions to complex problems. This approach combines expectations of the future with current reality. Use this approach only with an experienced creative thinking **group**.

●What-If: Future Fantasy Year

A very advanced creative thinking procedure that requires practice with your group.

Write your problem statement. How to...

Fantasize the future when someone solved your problem.
List each of the following items in turn on separate flip chart papers without thinking about the possible solution.

1. Non-evaluatively list those people inside and outside your school who gained by the success.

2. Non-evaluatively list those people who lost now that someone solved the problem.

3. Non-evaluatively list the 'Fantasy Resource People' who helped implement the solution. Include...

• Experts from the past and present.

• Experts from other colleges.

• Experts or animals from Sea World, Kennedy Space Center, or Epcot Center.

• Other experts or heroes, historical or mythological, from whom you want help.

• Fantasy helpers: writers, scientists, artists, inventors, thinkers, business students, professors, consultants, etc.

4. For each person or animal listed in #3 above, non-evaluatively list specifically what each uniquely does in the future to help implement the successful solution. Start each item with the name of the person or animal.

5. Use each activity listed in #4 above as a trigger-idea to spark new ideas to solve your problem as it exists today. Force combinations between these trigger-ideas and your problem statement.

6. Improve each idea using the idea-improvement triggers below.

Future fantasy year produces a cascade of trigger-ideas, thus:

People =>
    Unique activities =>
        Unexpected New & Useful ideas

Allow four to six hours for this very advanced trigger. Don't rush it because it seems non-logical. Logic will play a role, never fear. This creativity trigger: so powerful, an explosion of uniqueness.

TO ENHANCE CREATIVITY, IMPROVE YOUR IDEAS INNOVATIVELY

Once you select an idea, you can add to your creative output and innovation by improving it as much as you can. The idea-improving triggers described below helps you accomplish this creatively and may stimulate additional new ideas or provide new perspectives. Creative thinking soars as you creatively improve an idea.

Like-Improve Analysis

1. Write the idea.

2. Non-evaluatively list the characteristics and properties of the idea.

3. Non-evaluatively list what you like and what you find useful about the idea.

4. Non-Evaluatively list deficiencies that need improving. List these as How-to problem statements. How to...

5. Non-evaluatively list ways to overcome these deficiencies and improve the idea by responding to the How-to problem statements.

6. Recycle all the above until the idea works.

This procedure works very well even with the most bizarre ideas.

Improve Your Idea Imaginatively

Juggle the new idea in your mind until it clicks into place. Do it this way:

• Make it larger, greater, or extend and magnify it.
• Make it smaller, delete it, contract or diminish it.
• Rearrange it, adapt it, transpose it, or substitute for it.
• Consider it from a different point of view.
• Reverse it.
• Distort it.
• Make it stronger, taller, shorter, thicker, lighter, or weaker.
• Draw it.
• Sing it.
• Snort it
• Write a poem about it.
• Split it.
• Massage it.
• Combine and blend ideas.
• Sort them.
• Shuffle it.
• Turn up side down, backwards, opposite.

• Slice it into bits.
• Dance it.
• Make a metaphor of it.
• Imagine how it would work out and change it.
• Imagine what your favorite relative would say and modify the idea.
• Paint it.
• Eat it.
• Sleep on it.
• Lie on it.
• Roll it up.
• Stomp on it.
• Change its shape.
• Add to it.
• Announce it.
• Pronounce it.
• Print it.
• Analogize it.

• CHAPTER 18 •
BEEF UP MEETINGS WITH
CREATIVITY TRIGGERS

Creative thinking in meetings counts. Apply the advanced creativity triggers described in this book to regular meetings of your group. Use non-evaluative listing and **buzz groups** at least once in every meeting so everyone looks forward to being creative and solving problems when you get together.

Buzz Groups

Use this antidote to the quick fix during meetings. Especially useful when you want many ideas in a meeting without a long discussion.

One person presents a problem. Teams of four to six people turn in their seats to form small 'buzz groups' where they sit. Each buzz group quickly chooses a recorder, who non-evaluatively lists ideas on a writing pad for five minutes. The recorder quickly reads them aloud and gives the list to the presenter of the problem for future use. If the problem-presenter merely says, "Thank you" and does not get into a discussion, the total time takes less than fifteen minutes.

One variation: first ask the buzz groups to non-evaluatively list how-to problem statements. Then one or more of these are chosen by the presenter of the problem for the buzz group to use during idea generation. See Chapter 17 for an excellent use of buzz groups.

A TRUE STORY: In one of my workshops, a manager said he wanted to restructure work groups to eliminate the supervisors and have teams of workers led by temporary team leaders. Most people favored it except the local union, who insisted everyone get the same pay raise as the team leaders.

I formed three buzz groups with the 18 people present, and while they listed ideas, the plant manager and I privately agreed that, at most, he might get some trigger-ideas to spark ideas at some later time.

To our delight, the participants generated over 40 ideas, three of which when combined yielded a solution that he thought would satisfy the union, and because of its incentive orientation, he expected to increase productivity while reducing supervisor costs. The plant manager beamed. "Trust the process," we concluded

In addition, apply **reversal-dereversal** (described in Chapter 9) in your next regular meeting. Ask students to **reverse** the problem statement "How to stimulate creative thinking during our meetings" and non-evaluatively list ideas on "How to spoil creative thinking during our meetings."

This list often reflects what you usually do in meetings. Then dereverse each spoiler (as described in Chapter 9). Write "How to" in front of each idea and creatively smooth out each sentence into a sensible "How-to" problem statement.

For example, you could dereverse the spoiler, "Have domineering students present" into "How to stay creative with domineering students present" or into "How to keep students from dominating."

Reverse "Hold meetings at 4:45 on Friday" into "How to stay creative in a meeting held at 4:45 on Friday" or "How to avoid a meeting called at this time."

You will soon have many problem statements focusing on specific needs of your work group. Form buzz groups and non-evaluatively list solutions to the problem statements that impact the most. You all know best what spoils creativity during your meetings.

CREATIVITY SPOILERS IN MEETINGS

Some examples of creativity spoilers during meetings follow:
• People use quick negative criticism and judge ideas too soon.
• People don't freely share ideas.

- Highly vocal students dominate.
- Experts or high-ranking superiors overwhelm.
- Students lack training in creativity triggers.
- Leaders don't tell students that they want creative outcomes.
- Students do not stay interested and involved.
- Students focus on achieving the mission, not on new ideas.
- Students conceal emotions and inhibit spontaneity and humor.
- Students use win-lose methods, such as majority rules.
- Students select ideas prematurely, the quick fix.
- Students do not solve problems in structured ways.
- Students don't know the goals and purposes.
- Students use analytical and logical thinking too much.
- The leader picks ideas by verbal and nonverbal feedback.

CHECK THE SPOILERS THAT OCCUR IN YOUR MEETINGS

INCREASE CREATIVE THINKING DURING YOUR MEETINGS

In order to help creative thinking flourish during meetings.
- Use advanced problem-solving creativity triggers to:
  - Analyze problems creatively
  - Generate ideas abundantly
  - Select and combine ideas innovatively
  - Create trigger-proposals imaginatively
  - Develop workable solutions logically
  - Select proposals systematically
- Postpone evaluation and defer judgment of new ideas
- Establish a quota for many different ideas before selection
- When hearing a new idea, state what you like about the idea first
- Use effective team interaction triggers, such as:
  - Make decisions by consensus
  - Record on flip charts so all can see
  - Allow leadership roles to distribute naturally
  - Circulate the agenda before and action plans afterwards

- Rotate the chair among members of the team
- Discuss and review work group interactions frequently
- Review and discuss what spoils creative thinking
- Study the next page

CHECK THE BEHAVIORS THAT OCCUR IN YOUR MEETINGS

CHAIR MEETINGS TO HELP CREATIVE THINKING

1. Do not compete with other students to generate ideas. Support and build on the ideas of others.

(Leaders tend to favor their own ideas. This discourages contributions from other students.)

2. Respond non-evaluatively to new ideas. Create an atmosphere in which students consider all ideas.

(Responding in a non-evaluative way encourages everyone to participate.)

3. Do not permit anyone to be put on the defensive. Find value in all points of view. Start with what you like about what you heard.

(This approach encourages everyone to contribute and help new ideas.)

4. Get students to talk about the positives of an idea before the negatives. Do not kill an idea, just put it aside.

(This approach encourages everyone to contribute and help new ideas.)

5. Keep your energy level high.

(Your interest and alertness helps.)

6. Use every member of your work group. Talk to domineering students privately. Help quiet persons contribute.

(Everyone has unique, valuable ideas and information that contribute to quality outcomes.)

7. Record meetings and ask students with poor behavior to listen to the tape.

(This helps them change their behavior.)

8. Rotate the chair of the meeting.

(Being a follower and a leader leads to commitment and participation.)

9. Do not damage egos or self-esteem.

(This encourages everyone to share and leads to greater levels of participation.)

10. Defer judgment during idea generation and avoid early commitment to an idea.

(The leader has great power to sway members. This does not always result in choosing and developing the best idea.)

• CHAPTER 19 •
PERMANENT 'CREATIVITY GROUPS'

Permanent 'creative thinking groups' consist of students trained in diverse creativity triggers, and who can generate numerous problem statements and many ideas to help solve problems. They operate this way.

First: chose an experienced member as temporary head of the team to make the arrangements and act as recorder during the creative session. In addition, the head person will coach the problem-presenter in the roles he or she must play in order for the process to work and help the problem-presenter analyze the problem presented to the group.

Second: chose the five to eight members of the group. They provide the different perspectives to fuel the creative energy to generate endless How-to problem statements and new ideas. Their only reward: the inner fun of creative thinking and helping others to solve problems.

Finally: the problem-presenter must spend the time to clearly present the problem to the group. As an expert, the problem-presenter should stay non-evaluative and temporarily suspend judgment throughout to help the process work. A unique role of the problem-presenter: choose the problem statements for the group to tackle. No one else has this choice.

A TRUE STORY: I presented a one-day creative thinking workshop for a director and 33 of his managers. I formed six groups who worked on a problem presented by their director.

They helped analyze the problem by suggesting over 50 problem statements. He chose six of these, one for each group. They generated hundreds of ideas using non-evaluative listing, improve bizarre ideas game, idea gallery, and idea card.

They had a good time and the problem seemed on the way toward solution. Later, he asked me the best way to sort and select ideas.

WRITE YOUR PROBLEM AS PROBLEM-PRESENTER

1. Clarify whether your problem has to do with a situation, an individual, a group, or a thing?

2. Outline your problem. Make sure you have responsibility for the problem and can implement solutions.

Write a problem statement: How to...

3. Write I would like this problem resolved because...

4. List some possible indicators of success

5. List the resources available to help resolve the problem

6. List the obstacles you have to overcome

7. Note any deadlines

8. Include other issues

9. Write a broad-brush overview of your problem

10. List what you might lose if the problem continues

11. List what you will gain if you solve the problem

12. List the approaches and solutions you have already tried and why each has failed

13. List the benefits of the status quo and the advantages of doing nothing

14. Non-evaluatively list dozens of How-to problem statements and chose 2 to 4.

15. Summarize your problem in one How-to problem statement:
How to...

16. Whose problem?

17. What kind of problem?
School:
Students:

Financial:

Personal:

Other:

18. Scope

Funds:

Students:

Time:

Other Resources:

19. Indicate your gut feelings about the problem?

20. Include intangible Issues?

21. Include other issues?

List the criteria to select your How-to problem statement to give to the group.

CREATIVE THINKING GROUP SESSIONS

The sequence of creativity triggers and the time allotted for a session will vary with the importance of the problem. Sometimes a 60 minute buzz group session does the job. Sometimes you will need an entire day, or more, using many creativity triggers for defining problems and generating ideas. I find the following sequence of creativity triggers useful:

(1) The problem-presenter presents the problem.

(2) The recorder non-evaluatively lists the How-to problem statements suggested by the group. (Set a quota for 10-20 How-to statements.)

(3) The problem-presenter chooses the problem statement on which the group will focus.

(4) The recorder non-evaluatively lists the ideas suggested by the group. (Set a quota of 30-50 ideas.)

(5) The recorder non-evaluatively lists 10-15 bizarre trigger-ideas suggested by the group.

(6) The group combines and improves the most bizarre ideas.

(7) Each member of the group then sits quietly alone and writes ideas on 5x8 index cards, one idea per card (Idea Card).

(8) Give all the papers and cards to the problem-presenter.

(9) The group then uses 'like-improve analysis' to analyze how the group functioned. The recorder non-evaluatively lists what each person liked and what each wants improved to make the group even more effective.

During the session, the problem presenter
- presents a low profile
- does not act defensively
- does not put any idea down using statements, such as "we thought of that one" or "we tried that one"
- thanks everyone at the end for the excellent ideas generated
- answers an enthusiastic "yes" if asked if any of the ideas seem useful, an important reward for the group.

Use the problem-solving ladder and the triggers of creative thinking described in this book to achieve the highest quality solutions to the problem. Your creative thinking will soar as you use them on a regular basis. Enforce them by using them on important problems, especially recurring problems that lack clear focus. Ignite the creative flame within you, and keep lit with frequent use. Make creative thinking a daily, ongoing habit.

• CHAPTER 20 •
CREATIVITY REACH OUT

Now that you finished this book, what will you do? Hopefully, you know many creativity triggers, and found some of them useful…maybe even combined some of them. You may have planned to make their use permanent, that is, to use them throughout your career & life. If so, enjoy.

College Outreach

You can, of course, extend yourself now in a college outreach program, telling your classmates and friends about creativity triggers. I think you will help them a great deal if you do that and hope you agree.

Creativity Club

Indeed, you might form a student (& faculty) Creativity Club in your college. The Club can offer to teach creative thinking to students, staff, and faculty. It might help the college and community solve problems using creativity triggers in groups. A very worthy activity. What else do you think a Creativity Club might do?

Creativity Course

And you might even persuade a faculty member to sponsor a course on Creativity... Ah well, the stuff that dreams are made of...

THE 8-RUNG PROBLEM-SOLVING LADDER

Rung #1. Analyze Problems Creatively, the 1st Key Creative Rung On the Ladder
(Chapter 9)

Rung #2. Identify The Criteria To Select Your Problem Statement
(Chapter 10)

Rung #3. Choose The Final How-To Problem Statement(s)
(Chapter 11)

Rung #4. Generate New Ideas, the 2nd Key Creative Rung On The Ladder
(Chapter 12, alone; Chapter 17, in groups)

Rung #5. Combine Ideas Into Creative Trigger-Proposals, the 3rd key creative rung on the ladder
(Chapter 13)

Rung #6. Identify The Criteria To Choose Solutions
(Chapter 14)

Rung #7. Develop Sensible Workable Solutions
(Chapter 15)

Rung #8. Make Action Plans
(Chapter 16)

• PART 5 •
APPENDICES

• APPENDIX I •
USEFUL CREATIVITY TRIGGERS

"When you come up with the obvious, look elsewhere."

This appendix adapted from:
"Team Creativity At Work I & II: Creative Problem Solving At Its Best" by Ed Glassman (2010).

Students find advanced creativity triggers indispensable to achieving goals. What are your goals?

Creativity triggers marked with an *** indicates one of the key creative rungs.

***Rung #1.
Analyze the problem creatively.
Analogies & Metaphors
Essence or action verb
Fresh eye
Like-improve analysis
Needs, obstacles, and constraints
How-to statements
Problem's essence
Reversal-dereversal

Reverse assumptions
Weaknesses of quick-fix solutions
Who, what, where, when, and why
Why, why, why, why, and again, why
Word substitution

Rung #2.

Identify the criteria to select the right problem.

Rung #3.

Select one or more reasonable problem statements.

***Rung #4.

List many ideas and solutions.
Automatic writing
Bizarre trigger-ideas
Book pages as trigger-ideas
Brainstorming (Non-evaluative listing)
Brainwriting circles
Brainwriting clusters
Buzz groups
Combining ideas team
Dream-interruption brainwriting
Forced combinations
Free word association imagery
Future Fantasy Year
Idea card
Idea gallery
Idea grid
Improve bizarre trigger-idea game
Metaphors as trigger-ideas
Non-evaluative listing
Pictures as trigger-ideas
Quotations as trigger-ideas
Quota-setting for new ideas

Random words as trigger-ideas

Trigger-ideas

Weird to workable idea

***Rung #5.
Combine ideas into trigger-proposals innovatively.

Forced withdrawal

Idea board

New company

Return-to-reality

Trigger-proposals

Rung #6.
Identify the criteria to select appropriate proposals.

Rung #7.
Generate workable solutions.

Idea board

Rung #8.
Develop action plans.

Who does what, where, when, how, and why?

• APPENDIX II •
A CREATIVITY ADVENTURE
WITH NINE MAGIC DOTS

"Students experience a great deal of fun when creative. Not so much HA-HA fun as A-HA fun."

This appendix adapted from:
"Team Creativity At Work I & II: Creative Problem Solving At Its Best" by Ed Glassman (2010).

Nine Magic Dots

Many students, who know the following puzzle, think that it has only one answer. If you agree, prepare for a surprise. If you have seen it before, solve it anyway. Shift the paradigm and generate another quite different solution.

Here are nine magic dots.

```
O    O    O

O    O    O

O    O    O
```

The problem: Draw _four_ connecting straight lines that will touch all nine dots only once without lifting your pen or pencil from the paper.

If you have done it before, find a totally different solution. Spend at least five minutes before reading further.

If you did not solve the problem, what do you see when you look at the nine dots? If you see a square, or two triangles, or some other geometric figure, then you probably blocked your thinking with a familiar paradigm assuming boundaries that do not exist and staying within mind ruts that kept you inside the lines.

A HABIT THAT SPOILS CREATIVE THINKING: We often assume boundaries that may not exist. We stay within the lines. We think within the rules. We use unstated, phantom criteria. We use past company policies and attitudes as guidelines on how to do things without checking it out with others. We don't shift paradigms without permission.

You can connect these nine dots with **four** straight lines by moving outside the boundaries as shown here:

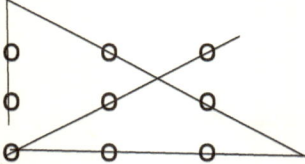

Do you like this answer? Do you think it elegant, the only one possible? Actually, the biggest assumed boundary of this problem comprises the unwarranted assumption that only one answer exists. In fact, you can find dozens of completely different answers to this problem; the one above constitutes a quick fix, the first adequate answer! How can we shift the paradigm and find the others?

Forced Withdrawal

We will use a very important, advanced creative thinking procedure I call 'forced withdrawal,' in which you forget the original problem and work to solve a distant version of it. In that way you may find new paradigms, new perspectives, and new solutions. The first forced withdrawal we shall consider is...

Here are the same nine magic dots.

```
O       O       O

O       O       O

O       O       O
```

The problem: This time use only _three_ connecting straight lines that touch each dot only once.

If you don't solve it, try to discover the mind ruts, assumed boundaries, unwarranted assumptions, and unstated criteria that block you.

First: What do you see when you look at the nine dots? I hope you kicked the habit of seeing a square or some other geometric figure. This time one block comes from seeing the nine dots on a piece of paper. For some solutions to this three-line problem, you need to perceive the nine dots as existing in space because the lines will leave the paper.

Second: Did you assume that the lines must go through the center of the dots? This unwarranted assumption also blocks you.

Third: How do you define a dot? In school, I learned that a dot represents a point in space with no dimension, without length, width or height. Those circles I call dots have length and width. Is that fair? Well, in real life, dots have length and width, and come in all sizes. On billboards, dots grow to the size of your head; and on clown costumes, polka dots fit the size of your shoe. So include reality in your definition of dots, lest you fall victim to another spoiler of creative thinking.

With expanded boundaries, clarified assumptions, and unrestricted definitions, we can solve the 9-dot, 3-line problem in this way:

Go off the paper, if necessary

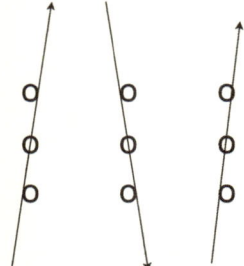

Go off the paper, if necessary

The first line merely touches the side of the first dot tangentially, passes through the center of the second dot, and again merely touches the side of the third dot tangentially. Extend the line as far as necessary, even off the paper. Do the same with the middle row of dots, and similarly with the third row of dots.

There's another solution based on non-Euclidean geometry which postulates that parallel lines meet at infinity. Using this perspective, the answer consists of three parallel lines, each of which touches a different row of dots, and then all three lines connect at infinity, a neat paradigm shift.

A HABIT THAT SPOILS CREATIVE THINKING: We only express 'fair' ideas, even before we select one. Don't let fairness spoil creative thinking in your head.)

Here's another **forced withdrawal** with the same nine magic dots.

```
O       O       O

O       O       O

O       O       O
```

The problem: Use only _two_ connecting straight lines that touch each dot only once.

Think it impossible? Check your assumed boundaries, unwarranted assumptions, unstated criteria, restricted definitions, mind ruts, and paradigms.

One block to this problem lies in your restricted definition of a line. In school, teachers define a line as a series of connected points that have only one dimension, length. In real life, lines have width. Look at traffic lines in the center of the road or lines of buses approaching an intersection. Again your habit of restricting definitions blocked you and led to the unwarranted assumption that you could use only thin lines.

Here's one answer to the 9-dot, 2-line problem: A wide line and a narrow line!

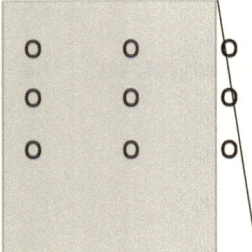

Try one last **forced withdrawal** with the same nine magic dots. **This time use only _one_ straight line that touches them all**. Find at least 15 answers before you continue reading...

Actually hundreds of acceptable solutions exist. The few solutions here will trigger new paradigms and viewpoints, and whet your appetite for more.

• Use one wide line that touches each dot.

• Run a large 3-dimensional line down through the nine dots from above so it passes through the paper, and touches each dot.

• Fold the paper so you can draw one line that touches each dot. (Did you assume you could not fold the paper?)

• Cut the paper so each dot is on a separate piece. Line up the pieces so one line touches each dot. (Did you assume you couldn't cut up the paper?)

• Twist the paper into a cone and draw a straight line that spirals around the surface of the cone and touches all nine dots. (Did you assume you couldn't twist the paper into a cone?)

• Put the paper with the nine dots on the equator of the earth and carefully draw a straight line that circles the earth enough times so it touches each dot. Or, put the paper on the edge of the universe and have your straight line circle the universe until it touches each dot.

(Did you assume you could not use fantasy? Note we expanded our mind-ruts from nine dots in a box to the edge of the universe).

• Write "ONE" over the top row of dots, "STRAIGHT" over the middle row of dots, and "LINE" over the bottom row of dots. You touched the dots with the words: "ONE STRAIGHT LINE." (Did you assume you could not use words?).

• Draw the line on the thin edge of the paper. View the nine dots through this side line.

• Move a straight line, like the windshield wiper on a car, and touch all dots. (Did you assume you couldn't move the line, or that the line had to touch all the dots at the same time?)

• Cut the line into 1,000 pieces and sprinkle it over the nine dots touching them all. (Did you assume you couldn't cut up the line?)

• Cut the paper so there is one dot on each piece of paper. Line up the dots on top of each other. Push a pencil through all the dots. You not only touched all the dots with one straight line, but you also annihilated the dots and the problem. About time, I'd say.

• Wait. Here's another solution to jolt your mind. Imagine you sit in my creative thinking workshop, and I merely say: "Touch each dot with only one straight line." Not write it, so you could see the spelling, but you only hear the words.

Would you bring in the king of beasts (or a picture of one) and cover the nine dots with one straight 'lion'? Or how about nine students named Dot eaten by one straight lion?

• I can't resist even more bizarre solutions. Change the dots into clothespins and hang them on one straight clothesline. (Did you assume that you could not convert the dots or the line into something else?)

• Or change the dots into tennis balls and play tennis with them until all have touched the tennis net made from one straight line. Or change the line into the shadow of a sun dial so it will eventually touch all the dots as the sun moves across the sky.

• Or convert the straight line into a sunbeam and use a glass prism to break it up into many colored lines that touch all nine dots. Had enough?

In my workshops on creative thinking, I always hear new and different solutions from the participants. See how many new solutions you can discover. Send me some through my website: http://creativity-for-college-students.weebly.com/

OR **http://www.r-and-d-creativity-innovation.com**

I always enjoy more.

NINE MAGIC DOTS CAN HELP THE CREATIVE CLIMATE OF YOUR MIND

You should realize by now that this puzzle represents a metaphor for all problems. You can learn a lot.

First: You may recall I stated my first answer for the nine-dot, four-line problem represented a quick fix, the first adequate answer. Here's why. You can apply many answers from the one-line problem to the four-line problem. How? Add three straight lines to the one straight line, thus:

$$\underline{\hspace{3cm}}/\vee$$

For example, use these four lines like a windshield wiper to solve the four-line problem. Did you assume all four straight lines had to touch a dot? Another unwarranted assumption!

Thus, we learn that even an excellent first answer mimics a quick fix, especially when students stop the creative thrust and fervor too soon. Note how effectively forced-withdrawal avoids the quick fix. We used forced withdrawal in Chapter 13.

Second: No one person in my workshops generates many of the solutions to the one-line problem. It was the sharing of mind ruts and paradigms that yielded numerous solutions, an important reason to use groups to solve problems.

Third: Each group in my workshops always generates unique solutions not generated by any other group. We would lose those solutions had that group not existed. The lesson learned: use more than one group to solve the same problem to produce a diversity of ideas and quality solutions.

Fourth: In my creative thinking workshops, some participants claim one solution is the best, or better than others. My response: you cannot tell until you know the criteria for an effective solution, and I never stated any criteria. Indeed, if you know the criteria before you generate ideas, you box in your imagination and evaluate each idea mentally against the criteria. In this way, you lose many ideas, especially trigger-ideas, and inhibit creative thinking for quality solutions.

You don't generate good or bad ideas. Ideas either fit or don't fit your stated criteria.

A HABIT THAT SPOILS CREATIVE THINKING: We list criteria to choose ideas before we list ideas and thereby limiting idea generation and diminishing quality solutions.

Do not make the criteria known before idea generation. Resist comparing ideas to the criteria and your imagination will soar. See Chapter 11 for what to do with prematurely presented criteria or phantom criteria that exist only in your mind.

Fifth: Old paradigms and unwarranted assumptions block most of the imaginative solutions to the nine-dot problem. Some of the **UNWARRANTED ASSUMPTIONS** that load down the nine-dot problem include:

• There's only one right answer.

- You must stay inside the square or the edge of the paper.

- Each line must touch and go through the center of at least one dot.

- Use Euclidian geometry only.

- Use only the mathematical definition of a dot or a line.

- Attach the lines only at their tips.

- Lines are not words spelled 'lion.'

- Lines are not phony-sounding cliches.

- You can't move or expand the dots, put them on a windshield; or convert them into popcorn, tennis balls, clothes lines, fishing hooks, or the names of students.

- You can't widen or cut up the lines, connect them in your mind, connect them using other lines, connect them along their lengths; or convert them in your mind into pencils, tennis nets, windshield wipers, clothes lines, fishing lines, fashion lines, movie lines, etc.

- You can't cut the paper, view it from the side, put it on the equator or the edge of the universe, fold it; or twist it into a cone or cylinder.

- You may only spell 'nine' only as 'n-i-n-e' and not as 'n-e-i-n.'

- Lines are rigid and permanent, not flexible, elastic, and temporary.

- Solutions must seem 'fair' and fit our unstated, phantom criteria.

- All lines must touch the dots at the same time.

Learn to detect unwarranted assumptions when approaching any problem. A little effort pays off greatly as your creative thinking soars.

• APPENDIX III •
WHICH CREATIVE TYPE ARE YOU ...
A 'DIGGER' OR A 'LEAPER'?

This appendix adapted from:
"Team Creativity At Work I & II: Creative Problem Solving At Its Best"
by Ed Glassman (2010).

DIGGERS & LEAPERS

Creative thinking, generating unexpected new ideas in the forefront, involves risk: risk of failure; risk that others will laugh, make fun, humiliate, and even ridicule. So the extent that students will conform to mainstream thinking determines how much they willingly risk. These traits, high or low risk taking, (high or low conforming), determines the kinds of creative outcomes your group can expect.

College groups insist on some level of conformity to norms, rules, customs, and policies. '**Digger**' types (high conformers) conform, analyze problems, and generate ideas along conventional paths, preferring solutions that stick to existing conditions. They make their creative output compatible with college norms and do not shift paradigms easily. Usually uncomfortable with the bizarre, they do not 'rock the boat.' They solve problems narrowly. Diggers do things **better**, not differently.

'**Leaper**' types (low conformers), the opposite of diggers, leap around in their thinking. They prefer to shift paradigms broadly and explode their thoughts beyond reasonable boundaries of the original problem. They love the bizarre and enjoy 'rocking the boat.' They solve problems innovatively. Leapers do things **differently**, not just better.

You have to remind **high-conforming diggers** to 'think outside the box.' On the other hand, a **low-conforming leaper** doesn't even perceive the box.

Does this seem familiar? Here we have two opposing types in conflict over style, each style affecting how students shift paradigms; analyze problems; and generate, select, and develop ideas. Two opposing types about the acceptance of change itself.

Extreme diggers or leapers don't exist normally in college, even if you think you know one. Locate yourself or other students on the scale between the extremes. The following may help:

Circle how close you come to resemble a **digger** on the following scale:

Low   1 2 3 4 5   High

Diggers, high conformers, reliable and efficient, tend toward precision. They solve problems in conventional ways and don't shift paradigms very much. They seek stability. Other students see them as safe and dependable. They put in long hours on detailed work without boredom and challenge rules only with strong support from others. They comply. Diggers, sensitive to other students, work to maintain group cohesion, teamwork, and cooperation. On the scale of 1 to 5 above, how **closely** do these traits fit you (or another)?

Do high conformers prove useful in a group? Of course they do. Without them, chaos occurs, and little gets finished. A group without enough diggers falls apart, since high conformers provide the necessary glue that holds things together.

Circle how close you come to resemble a **leaper** on the following scale:

Low   1 2 3 4 5   High

Leapers, low conformers, on the other hand, tend to lack discipline. They shift paradigms frequently and approach problems from new angles. They challenge a problem's assumptions and analyze a problem incessantly. They don't comply easily. Their indifference to group consensus leads others to see them as abrasive, undependable, impractical, or combative. Routine tasks bore them. They challenge rules frequently, and have little respect for past customs. Insensitive to other students and group cohesion, they don't cooperate. On a scale of 1 to 5, how **close** do these preferences fit you (or another)?

Do leapers prove valuable? Of course they do! A group without enough leapers staggers toward complacency and stagnation, and can expect difficulty the next time the environment changes.

The digger or leaper styles have little to do with creative ability. Both types seem equally creative within their style. Still, students perceive leapers as more creative because they take bigger risks, have a more adventurous spirit, and use bizarre trigger-ideas during problem-solving.

A **third** type exists, students in the **middle** range of conformance who span the gap between high and low conformers. These moderate students can, within limits, act as moderate diggers or leapers, and can communicate with both extremes. The moderate conformers of a group usually include its leader, since leaders must communicate with all types. Again, this has no bearing on creative ability, but reflects a preference for moderation.

The extreme types have much to say about each other. Diggers say low conformers act weird, too difficult to work with, too undependable, and they don't want to work with them. They'll say, "He took an important assignment and developed a brilliant solution to a problem I never gave him." (Interestingly, leapers say the same thing about other leapers, effectively isolating themselves from most students.)

In contrast, leapers say diggers act like sticks in the mud and red tape bureaucrats, uptight, narrow-minded students who spoil everyone's creative thinking. As expected, leapers say they do not want to work with diggers (or leapers).

Low And High Conformers Can Help Each Other

Help leapers and diggers respect each other's unique contributions. Get them to recognize each other's value and understand that each type does necessary jobs that the other dislikes. The digger loves digging in one place, while the leaper abhors it. The leaper loves to leap around, nibbling here and there, looking for the best place to dig. Not so the digger. Thus you need both types to succeed, and you need to act like a moderate conformer to manage them.

Discuss this openly. Make leapers and diggers aware of their importance to produce quality outputs. Make them proud of what they uniquely accomplish and contribute. After all, the high conformer provides the solid foundation for the leaper's risky activities, while the digger provides the impetus for periodic change to avoid complacency and stagnation. Thus, when collaborating, high conformers supply stability and continuity, while low conformers supply the break with past traditions and accepted norms. Excellence results from collaboration between both types.

A TRUE STORY: After I discussed this theory about low and high conformers in a workshop, one person told me about an associate working on a problem for over two years with no progress, probably a low conformer working on a problem that needed a high conformer.

Six weeks later, I presented another workshop at the same location, and the same person told me that I had saved them a "bundle" of money. Apparently they "switched the nibbler (a low conformer) with a digger (a high conformer) and made more progress in six weeks than in the previous 2 1/2 years."

• APPENDIX IV •
HOW TO RELATE TO
CREATIVE LOW CONFORMERS

"You have to remind **high-conforming diggers** to 'think outside the box.' On the other hand, a **low-conforming leaper** doesn't even perceive the box."

This appendix adapted from:
"Team Creativity At Work I & II: Creative Problem Solving At Its Best" by Ed Glassman (2010).

Most students relate to diggers relatively easily. High conformers work well in groups and cooperate with policies and norms. Leapers require different approaches.

You need leapers to escape routine complacency in your groups. With some exceptions, leapers tend to stay loners and need special conditions to operate effectively.

A leaper, as a group member, clashes when working with logical, linear thinkers. Leapers suffocate in rigid cultures, cause distress to other students, and they perceive others as destructive to their creative efforts.

They become impatient with routine, repetitive jobs, and this often results in premature task termination. They irritate or alienate other students with their intense drive, their focus on 'pet' projects and their idiosyncrasies. Student colleagues often perceive them as self-serving loners and disruptive to group's efforts. Leapers can suffer from loneliness, isolation, and rejection.

Every leaper exists as a majority of one. Easily bored, they would rather move into untried areas, not worried about risk or troubled by ambiguity. Uninterested in social matters, they may lack social skills.

They want to use their minds to solve difficult, personally fulfilling problems. When working in unexplored areas, they do well without support or approval from others.

Getting along with leapers in your group requires a capacity for patience and good will. Some approaches make it a little easier, but do not expect miracles. Bright low conformers can overwhelm.

• Let your low conformers help you and the group get out of routine complacency.

• Make sure low conformers know the objectives of the group so they work toward similar goals.

• Tolerate their honesty.

• Let low conformers know that you consider them respected, valuable members of the group.

• Accept the low conformer's firm stance without calling them stubborn.

• Help the low conformers in your group see the progress they have made when depressed and discouraged.

• Do not interpret their continual dissatisfaction as disloyalty.

• Appreciate the low conformer's bizarre ideas.

• Tolerate the low conformers' flow of ideas without asking them to settle on one too early, the quick fix.

• Do not burden the low conformers in your group with suggestions that slow them down when hot on the trail of a solution.

• Accept the low conformer's independence and do not take offense when they proceed without asking your advice.

- Help prevent them from frustrating other students.

- Interact with low conformers informally.

- Get their input but don't try to make them a team player.

- Accept the low conformer's fantasies and do not accuse them of being unrealistic.

- Help low conformers sell their proposals and make them relevant.

- Respect their periods of isolation.

- Give them encouraging feedback concerning their ideas.

- Help provide the kinds of interactions they need.

- Help low conformers feel secure so they risk creative effort.

- Support low conformers when others criticize them.

- Give low conformers enough time for the incubation process to work.

- Provide low conformers in your group the support needed during the depressing episodes of the creative process.

Make an action plan that you think would help...

WHO ...?

DOES WHAT...?

WHEN...?

WHERE...?

HOW...?

And WHY...?

1. Share books and articles on creative thinking during luncheon discussion groups.

2. Expect yourself and everyone to use advanced creativIty triggers to shift paradigms and solve problems creatively.

3. Provide workshops on advanced creativity triggers.

4. Bring in guest speakers and creativity consultants now and then.

5. Foster and stress the enjoyment of creative effort.

6. Devise meetings that let people freewheel and flow easily with new ideas.

7. Stop criticizing new ideas too soon.

8. Allow people enough time for creative thinking.

9. Stop your habitual automatic NO toward new ideas.

10. When focusing on creative work, mentally resist and immunize yourself against the lures of future rewards. Instead, concentrate on the immediate pleasure and enjoyment.

11. Relentlessly squeeze out alternative ideas.

12. Transform old ideas into new ones:
    Recombine, magnify, distort, reverse, add to, subtract from, reduce, condense, expand, delete, digress, manipulate, twist, entwine, titillate, weaken, fantasize, meditate, daydream, put aside, connect, assemble, disconnect, reassemble, take apart, free associate, etc.

13. Incubate a lot with your shoes off.

14. Use bizarre trigger-ideas to stimulate new ideas.

15. Raise your level for tolerating low conformity for offbeat clothes, ideas, and behaviors in your college.

16. Reduce the fear of failure in someone who suggests something different.

17. Install an 'idea gallery' outside your door to keep people informed about problems that need creative solutions.

18. Consult a wide range of people when analyzing a problem.

19. Encourage combining ideas during problem solving.

20. Don't comment that more than 10 ideas exist here. Such quick negative criticism over such a trivial issue spoils creativity.

In order for you to assess the factors shown to affect creative thinking, please evaluate your skills using the five-point scale below.

0. I never do this.
1. I rarely do this.
2. I sometimes do this.
3. I frequently do this.
5. I always do this.
    Please note no rating of 4 exists.

DIRECTIONS: Circle the number that you think applies to you.
Example for practice:
I want to think more creatively.　　　　　　　 0　1　2　3　5

A. CLIMATE AND HABITS

I buffer myself from interruptions during creative thinking sessions.
　　　　　　　　　　　　　　　　　　　　　 0　1　2　3　5
I exchange ideas with other people.　　　　 0　1　2　3　5
I know when I need creative thinking.　　　　 0　1　2　3　5
I avoid quick, negative criticism and an automatic No when I generate new ideas and proposals.　　　　 0　1　2　3　5
I avoid assuming boundaries and making unwarranted assumptions that box me in when I want to shift paradigms and solve problems

creatively.   0 1 2 3
5

I allocate enough time for creative thinking, for incubation, and for using creativity triggers during problem solving.

                                                                  0 1

2 3 5

I state positive things about a new idea or proposal before I state the difficulties to overcome.   0 1 2 3 5

I want to solve problems creatively as an ongoing, daily activity.
                                                               0 1 2 3 5

I exhibit spontaneity and humor during problem solving.
                                                               0 1 2 3 5

I review and discuss how the climate and my habits affect my creative thinking for problem-solving.   0 1 2 3 5

I take risks and do not punish myself for expected failure. I learn from failure.   0 1 2 3 5

I value "thinking time" as well as "doing things."   0 1 2 3 5

B. CREATIVITY TRIGGERS

I use analogies, metaphors, like-improve analysis, and guided fresh eye to analyze problems innovatively.   0 1 2 3
5

I use a variety of advanced creativity triggers to define problems, enhance idea generation, and combine ideas into trigger-proposals that spark quality solutions.   0 1 2 3 5

I identify criteria to select ideas **after** idea generation, not before.
                                                               0 1 2 3 5

I review and discuss how advanced creativity triggers help shift paradigms and solve problems.   0 1 2 3 5

I generate bizarre trigger-ideas, and use them to spark better ideas to solve problems.   0 1 2 3 5

I select and combine ideas into creative trigger-proposals before I generate solutions.   0 1 2 3
5

I use many creativity triggers to define problems before I generate ideas. 0 1 2 3 5

I set quotas for ideas before I generate them. 0 1 2 3 5

While I generate ideas, I postpone evaluation and defer judgment.

0 1 2 3 5

I use many idea-generating triggers, like brainwriting, future fantasy year, trigger-ideas, idea card, etc. 0 1 2 3 5

I separate analyzing problems, generating ideas, and combining ideas into three creative rungs during problem-solving.

0 1 2 3 5

I obtain on-going training on using advanced creativity triggers.

0 1 2 3 5

C. STRUCTURES

I set deadlines that allow plenty of time for creative thinking during problem solving. 0 1 2 3 5

I obtain outside stimulation attending seminars led by experts in areas other than my own. 0 1 2 3 5

I seek resource-help everywhere to help my creative thinking.

0 1 2 3 5

I review how my personal creativity environment helps or spoils my creative thinking at work. 0 1 2 3 5

I attend workshops on advanced creativity triggers.

0 1 2 3 5

I fill and renew my mind with new information for creative solutions by attending professional meetings and trade fairs, and by talking to experts, and reading, etc. 0 1 2 3 5

D. HELP FROM OTHERS

I review and discuss how other people help or spoil my creative thinking. 0 1 2 3 5

I like collaborating with other people. 0 1 2 3 5

E. MOTIVATION FOR CREATIVE THINKING AND RISK-TAKING

I motivate myself to stay creative.   0 1 2 3 5

I focus on my daily enjoyment and the fun of my work, rather than the long-term rewards.   0 1 2 3 5

I motivate myself to shift paradigms and solve problems creatively because of the enjoyment.   0 1 2 3 5

Rewards seem fair.   0 1 2 3 5

I volunteer for assignments.   0 1 2 3 5

I become involved in the challenge of solving problems creatively, the daily enjoyment in the work, and the joy of solution.   0 1 2 3 5

I have high stability to encourage risk-taking.   0 1 2 3 5

I solve problems creatively for self-satisfaction and enjoyment.
                    0 1 2 3 5

I learn from failure and do not punish myself for it.   0 1 2 3 5

I review and discuss how effectively I motivate myself for creative thinking and risk taking.   0 1 2 3 5

F. TOLERANCE FOR LOW CONFORMITY

I have a high level of tolerance for borderline behavior in other people.
                    0 1 2 3 5

I respect people at work with different lifestyles.   0 1 2 3 5

I express ideas outside the mainstream thinking.   0 1 2 3 5

I have a high level of tolerance for humor.   0 1 2 3 5

I make accommodation for the social graces of loners, extroverts, low and high conformers, introverts, and innovators.   0 1 2 3 5

I decorate and individualize my work area.   0 1 2 3 5

I dress as I wish.   0 1 2 3 5

I use the unique strengths of other people and ignore differences that do not contribute to effectiveness.   0 1 2 3 5

I review and discuss how my tolerance for low and high conformity helps or spoils creative thinking.　　　　　　　　　　0　1　2　3　5

I tolerate low-conforming ideas and proposals.　　0　1　2　3　5

I don't take issue with beards, mustaches, and hair styles.

　　　　　　　　　　　　　　　　　　　　0　1　2　3　5

I value the creative low conforming person and the creative high conforming person, and I accommodate both types.　　0　1　2　3　5

Messages To Yourself About Your Creative Output

a) Please list what you like about your creative output:

b) Please list things you do that help increase your creative output:

c) Please list things that would help you increase your creative output if you were to do them more frequently or more skillfully (please specify which):

d) Please list things that would help you increase your creative output if you did them less frequently or to stop doing them (please specify which):

e) Please list what you want to improve in your creative output at work:

Follow-up

After you discover how you operate creatively, diagnose how effectively you help your own creative effort. Note especially items you marked "0" and "1." These may be your major roadblocks.

Analyze the problems you discover, generate ideas, develop workable solutions and sensible action plans. Especially focus on and solve problems associated with items marked "0" and "1.

• APPENDIX VII •
SOME RESEARCH ON CREATIVITY AT WORK

Adapted from:
"Team Creativity At Work I & II: Creative Problem Solving At Its Best"
by Ed Glassman (2010).

Before my workshop on creativity, I asked participants to fill out a questionnaire so I could fine-tune the workshop to their specific needs.

About 450 people in R&D, marketing, and manufacturing in six Fortune-500 companies responded. To appreciate their answer to one question, please write your response before reading further:

When I am creating, I feel...

Almost all respondents said they had good feelings: they used words like excited, fulfilled, joyful, good, enthusiastic, insightful, stimulated, enjoyable, intense, fun, happy, delighted; they wrote staying creative made them feel good, satisfied, useful, energetic, alert; other answers included challenged, worthwhile, energized.

About 3% listed negative feelings, such as feeling anxious, frustrated, timid, stressed, disturbed, bothered, mainly because of anticipated negative reactions from colleagues.

Learn from these comments to lead your team more effectively. **First**, encourage enjoyment and satisfaction in work to help people stay creative as problem solvers on the job and boost creative outcomes.

Second, use the sheer enjoyment of creative thinking to provide an inner reason for your people to stay creative. Help people focus their daily work on the instant enjoyment and fun inherent in creative thinking.

A manager told me about one leader who greeted his people with: "Are you having fun today?" If they answered yes, he asked them to share the fun with him. If they answered no, he asked what he could do to help them have fun.

Use the approach: "Are you having fun today?" to focus people on their inner motivators and the desire to stay creative: the good feelings, the enjoyment and the fun that people report feeling when they create.

Third, apply the elements of responses to new ideas described in Chapter 7.

Let us continue with responses to the other statements in my pre-workshop questionnaire. Please jot down your own responses to:

"The biggest help to my creative thinking at work..."

"The biggest obstacle to my creative thinking at work..."

"I need the following from my job environment to stay more creative..."

The main responses from 93 R&D chemists and engineers to the statement in my questionnaire: "The biggest help to my creative thinking at work is..." including the actual numbers of R&D chemists and engineers who mentioned this item (see table below):

THE BIGGEST HELP TO MY CREATIVE THINKING AT WORK IS....

	R&D Chemists & Engineers
a. Support and encouragement from other people	25
b. Sharing ideas with other people	17
c. Time	14
d. Challenging task; adventurous feelings	11
e. Freedom	8
f. Being alone	8
g. Perceived a problem to be solved	7
h. Rewards, credit, acknowledgment	5
i. Miscellaneous	9

Forty-two (combined items a and b above) of these chemists and engineers (almost half) mentioned interaction with other people as the biggest help to their creative thinking at work.

Surprisingly, freedom did not rank first (item e), and eight people listed 'being alone.' (item f). One conclusion: Leaders need to treat people differently so all types become self-motivated to stay creative. Adopt the attitude that everyone gets special treatment at work.

I found similar results in a Fortune-500 company involving 20 R&D managers, 32 R&D supervisors, and 24 of their subordinates who responded to "The biggest help to my creative thinking is....." as follows (see the Table below):

THE BIGGEST HELP TO MY CREATIVE THINKING AT WORK IS....

	20 R&D Managers	32 R&D Supervisors	24 Scientists & Engineers
Support and encouragement from other people	4	5	5
Sharing ideas with others	6	7	12
Supervision	0	0	4
Time	6	11	2
Challenge	1	1	0
Freedom	5	9	4
Being alone	1	1	1
Perceived a problem to be solved	0	0	0
Rewards, recognition, acknowledgment	0	0	0
Overcoming personal limitations	1	3	0
Resources	0	0	2
My internal resources	0	0	4

(The totals exceed the number of people, since some people wrote more than one thing.)

Again no one listed rewards. They wrote support, encouragement, and sharing ideas with other people as the biggest help; they also listed time and freedom. The similarity between these and the responses above strikes me as significant.

Lest you think only R&D personnel respond this way, I present a summary of how 54 non-R&D people responded: Other people (36); Time (7); Climate (8); Challenge (3); Freedom (4); Miscellaneous (4). This sample includes mostly managers and professionals in marketing, human resources, and manufacturing from 34 Fortune-500 companies. Again no one mentioned rewards.

I categorized responses from 24 managers in three large International Fortune-500 Companies in England as: Other people (12); Freedom (6); Challenge (2); Time (2), Climate (2); Understand job (2); Rewards (1); Miscellaneous (3). Though few in number, these people appear similar to managers and professionals in the United States.

Interestingly, no one mentioned vendors or customers as the biggest help to creative thinking. Not using customers in this way does not fit the stated goals of these market oriented firms. One lesson: Use vendors to help creative output since vendors do want to help.

One R&D scientist actually wrote: "The biggest help to my creativity is ... when my boss leaves town. Was he writing about you?

Overall, these results indicate that many people perceive that other people provide the biggest help to their creative thinking. This provides an important clue on how team leaders can spur creative output.

First: Encourage and build in activities so people interact more frequently, exchanging and discussing each other's ideas.

Second: Bring in an occasional expert professional to help people's ideas.

Third: Arrange for more creative thinking in small groups during regular meetings. For example, make it a norm that buzz groups define and generate ideas to help solve at least one problem in every meeting of your work group, as described in Chapter 12 of my book. This will help the exchange of ideas and enhance creative thinking.

"The Biggest Obstacle in My Job Environment To
My Creative Thinking..."

What blocks creative thinking at work? A few people mentioned personal limitations, newness to the job, lack of creative thinking skills, etc.

However, almost all the comments from the 450 respondents included conditions you can control: lack of time; lack of freedom; abundance of quick negative criticism; distractions; low encouragement; low acceptance of new ideas; ineffective meetings. Some wrote about cautious management styles; red tape; lack of appreciation; unsuitable rewards.

Others blamed limited resources; overload of work; interruptions; demands of others; the need to stay productive rather than creative; limited communication; mountains of paperwork.

The good news: you can correct most of these in the workplace.

"I Need The Following From My Job Environment
To Be More Creative..."

What stimulates on-the-job creative thinking? The 450 respondents concentrated on: more talking to others; more time; more freedom; less red tape, paperwork and routine jobs; better resources; more respect as a professional; more recognition for innovation; better communications; an atmosphere that encourages originality; fewer meetings; better teamwork; fewer penalties for failure; fewer interruptions; more supportive atmosphere.

As one person wrote: "the opportunity to be heard, openness, more participation in selection of assignments, more freedom in selection of approaches, less daily and weekly accounting of activity."

If you want to find out what spoils creative thinking or how to stimulate creative output in your group, ask your people either directly or through questionnaires. Create your own questionnaires.

If this process overwhelms you, obtain the help of consultants who can facilitate the process and ensure favorable outcomes.

• APPENDIX VIII •
ANTI-CREATIVITY FORCES
vs
CREATIVITY TRIGGERS

Anti-creativity forces are in constant array against creativity triggers, Even though being creative is a natural state for humankind (we could not have survived and flourished without it), anti-creativity forces surround us and reduce our capacity to think creatively and produce high quality creative output.

Where are these anti-creativity forces? We can see anti-creativity forces operating in children, bright creative preschool youngsters, who slowly lose their creative edge as they grow older. 'Rules' are anti-creativity, and yet we must instill some societal restraint, else chaos result.

We see anti-creativity forces in how negatively we greet new ideas, killing them swiftly, though sometimes kindly.

We see anti-creativity forces operating when we lure people away from their daily enjoyment of creative effort with long-range external rewards, such as, salary raises, promotions, medals, etc.

And we see anti-creativity forces marshaling their strength against creativity triggers when people do not take responsibility to create a creative environment.

Finally, we see anti-creativity forces when people avoid the 8 rung problem-solving ladder and make no effort to learn or use the advanced, focused creativity triggers that prop the sequence up and help it succeed.

Anti-creativity forces are not evil. They are us. They are cultural mind-ruts and very difficult to weed out.

How to defeat the anti-creativity forces? One way to slip out of this difficulty: use the 8 rung problem-solving ladder, and allow the sequence to lead you to a solution that works for you. Thus, creativity triggers provide the mechanism to win against the anti-creativity forces.

Perhaps you could read this book again and take note where you aid the anti-creativity forces through your own mind-ruts, and help anti-creativity forces triumph. Instead, affirm your intention to use the creativity triggers more often and on more problems.

Make the creative process a daily, ongoing habit.

ANTI-CREATIVITY FORCES vs CREATIVITY TRIGGERS

CREATIVITY TRIGGER	*ANTI-CREATIVITY FORCE*
1. Receiving new ideas in a supportive, non-evaluative manner. ("Let's improve that idea.")	1. Receiving new ideas in a non-supportive, evaluative manner. ("That idea is no good.")
2. Focusing on the daily enjoyment of creative effort, the internal reward.	2. Focusing on long-range external rewards, such as, salary raises, promotions, medals, etc.
3. Learning and using advanced, targeted creativity triggers, such as, brainstorming, brainwriting, forced combinations, fresh eye, How to, metaphors and analogies, future fantasy, idea card, idea grid, etc.	3. Not learning, not using, and avoiding advanced, targeted creativity triggers.
4. Seeking to discover and use personal environmental creativity triggers.	4. Not seeking and avoiding personal environmental creativity triggers.
5. Enjoying and welcoming bizarre ideas as triggers to better ideas.	5. Avoiding and squelching the use of bizarre ideas.
6. Taking 100% responsibility to create a climate conducive to creative effort.	6. Taking no responsibility for a creative climate.
7. Learn and use the 8 rung problem-solving ladder to attack problems creatively.	7. Ignore and avoid the problem-solving ladder.

CREATIVITY TRIGGER	ANTI-CREATIVITY FORCE
8. Seek many alternatives to avoid the quick fix.	8. Jump right into the quick fix by selecting the first adequate idea.
9. Listen to and get inspired by other people's ideas.	9. Stay away from other people.
10. Seeing things through a fresh perspective; forced withdrawal, fresh eye, etc.	10. Staying sharply focused and avoiding different paradigms and points of view.
11. Spend time incubating the problem and thinking about it.	11. No thinking time alloted for incubation.
12. Examining dogma (the 'box')	12. Being unaware of, and accepting dogma as truth.
13.	13.
14.	14.
15.	15.
16.	16.
17.	17.

LIST YOUR OWN ANTI-CREATIVITY FORCES & CREATIVITY TRIGGERS

• APPENDIX IX •
FORCED COMBINATIONS
FOR THE ARTS

Assume you work in the arts ...

painting, sculpture, choreography, poetry, short stories, mysteries, plays, musicals, music, etc.

Assume further that you are blocked in the creative aspects of your work, and attempts at non-evaluative listing and non-evaluative writing have failed to get you back on track.

What to do? Fear not. A creativity trigger awaits. However, you really have to want this to work for it to help.

Here's how. For example, you are a painter and you are blocked. (What follows applies to all the arts.)

1. Select two paintings you like (painting 'A' and painting 'B').

2. Non-evaluatively list attributes and elements of each painting separately.

3. Design a painting combining the attributes and elements of the two paintings ('A' and 'B') into one design (painting 'X').

4. Select two other paintings (C and D) and treat them the same way you treated paintings 'A' and 'B,' producing a design for painting 'Y.'

5. Now list elements and attributes separately for painting designs 'X' and 'Y.'

6. Design a painting combining the attributes and elements of the two paintings ('X' and 'Y') into one design (painting 'Z').

7. Decide which of the new designs you want to paint, and do so.

The paradigm diagrams like this:

$$\text{'A'+'B'} \quad \text{'C'+'D'}$$
$$\downarrow \qquad\qquad \downarrow$$
$$\text{'X'} \quad + \quad \text{'Y'}$$
$$\downarrow$$
$$\text{'Z'}$$

The same creativity trigger applies to the other arts with appropriate adjustments. Your creative block might end provided you want it.

Remember that I am on your side. Please let me know how it works out. Please contact me through my **website**:
http://creativity-for-college-students.weebly.com/

SOME COMMENTS FROM OTHERS

Email from my granddaughter, Sarah, January 28, 2011.

Your book sounds like a great idea! I think a lot of college students are lacking in creative ideas.

By my senior year, I definitely felt as though I had run out of anything even resembling creativity.

Are these creative ideas solely for academic purposes, or do they include ideas for recreational activities on Saturday afternoon as well?

What a great idea!

Sarah

Email from another grandchild, January 21, 2011.

I'm not sure I'm a good source for your creativity question, I'm not creative at all (as the art projects I've made with you guys can attest, ha ha.

ED GLASSMAN, THE AUTHOR, IN HIS 80TH YEAR

www.ingramcontent.com/pod-product-compliance
Lightning Source LLC
Chambersburg PA
CBHW020417290526
45785CB00002B/602